W9-BMP-872

Some words about

Voices *of the*
HEART

"Timing is everything!" On my journey through life, I've experienced stretches of joy and peace, signs of success and accomplishment. When my life was slowing recently, Linda's *Voices of the Heart* came my way. At that juncture, tempted to say: "I can't," I found myself inspired by her story to say: "I want to!" And the choice was mine!

—Rev. George Bergin, svd,
spiritual director, /
Duxbury, Massachusetts

An inspirational read...viewed in terms of Chinese philosophy. Linda's struggle in life's journey is to approximate the balance by which we attain health and fulfillment. She finally makes the most important decision of her journey and discovers a beautiful balance that two can share.

—Ken Branco, Lic. Ac.,
acupuncture healthcare,
Westport, Massachusetts

> Every
> moment
> of light
> and dark is
> a miracle.
> Walt Whitman

Voices *of the*
HEART

I wish you peace!

Voices *of the* HEART

A Journey of Faith, Hope, & Love

Linda Lambert Pestana
with D.K. Llorens

TATE PUBLISHING *& Enterprises*

Voices of the Heart
Copyright © 2009 by Linda Lambert Pestana. All rights reserved.

No part of this publication may be reproduced, stored in a retrieval system or transmitted in any way by any means, electronic, mechanical, photocopy, recording or otherwise without the prior permission of the author except as provided by USA copyright law.

Scripture quotations marked (NASB) are taken from the *New American Standard Bible®*, Copyright © 1960, 1962, 1963, 1968, 1971, 1972, 1973, 1975, 1977, 1995 by The Lockman Foundation. Used by permission.

The opinions expressed by the author are not necessarily those of Tate Publishing, LLC.

Published by Tate Publishing & Enterprises, LLC
127 E. Trade Center Terrace | Mustang, Oklahoma 73064 USA
1.888.361.9473 | www.tatepublishing.com

Tate Publishing is committed to excellence in the publishing industry. The company reflects the philosophy established by the founders, based on Psalm 68:11,
"The Lord gave the word and great was the company of those who published it."

Book design copyright © 2009 by Tate Publishing, LLC. All rights reserved.
Cover design by Kellie Southerland
Interior design by Stephanie Woloszyn

Published in the United States of America

ISBN: 978-1-61566-290-6
1. Biography & Autobiography / Personal Memoirs
2. Biography & Autobiography / Religious
09.11.02

Dedication

This book is dedicated in love and with love ...
... to my mother for blessing me with life;
the power of love; wisdom; and true beauty;
and the greatest gift of all,
my faith.

... to my husband, Louis, for sharing my life,
his tender love, gentleness,
and total support of my dreams.

Acknowledgments

Sometimes simple words say it best. May these expressions of gratitude touch the many hearts that have blessed my life throughout my journey with *Voices of the Heart*.

First, I give gratitude to the God of my life. I could do nothing without God's inner whispers and constant love and compassionate help.

To Debra Llorens, my friend and editor, for her unending belief in this project. Debi found the voice to my thoughts and feelings. No one else could have guided my memoir with more insight, conviction, diligence, and love. My deepest gratitude to a real visible earth angel.

To those at Tate Publishing, *Voices of the Heart* has a true home with you. How blessed I am to have you walk this journey with me. Thank you to one and all for your support and guidance.

I am grateful to Don Langevin for always having believed in me and for blessing me with the courage to move forward.

To my dear friend and author, Gilda Arruda, for her unending encouragement, support, and love.

To my dear family: Claire, Judy, Cora, and Charlie, and

in loving memory of my brother Bobby and sister Carol. You have each touched my heart with your forever love, which has been a real inspiration to me. Your love and support has truly set the stage for who I am today. I love, honor, and cherish each one.

To the many people I have met along the way, along with the many people whose names do not appear on this page, but their love, friendship, and support are forever written into my heart.

To my dear daughter, Jennifer; her husband, Jonathan; and our little Julia, you light up my life. I am so grateful for your love and support. You are my shining stars.

To my husband, Louis, a tender and loving thank you for walking this incredible endeavor along with me, for your unflinching support and encouragement. For reminding me to smile often and to laugh much; this gift still keeps on giving. You are forever my hero. I love you.

Contents

Preface

Sharing my story has been a journey inward, and, as is true of most introspection, it was not easy. Revisiting unwanted emotions and difficult situations was tantamount to walking naked on these pages, exposing the shameful feelings and memories of the past. However, I am convinced that if I remain faithful and honest, as well as somewhat vulnerable, others will draw comfort, courage, and strength by seeing something of their own lives reflected in mine.

The gift of this effort is that by recalling both pleasant as well as painful memories the process of healing and wholeness will gradually unfold. In the process of traveling down these roads of reflection, today I am somehow different than when I first began this amazing journey.

I hope and pray that as you, dear reader, move deeper into your own journey, you will gain greater clarity and a stronger sense of your own vitality of soul. May you awaken to the beauty in yourself, in others, and in life.

From my heart and soul,

Linda

Chapter 1

The Beginning

> **Go where it hurts.**
>
> **Step into the broken places of pain, fear, and confusion.**

The complexity of my emotional life began at birth. I was born but not wanted. I felt loved but never lovable. I tried to be good, kind, and loving but never felt good enough, kind enough, or loving enough. Of course, Mom never expressed these thoughts to me, but I believe I was born with the scars that come only when one imagines that one lacks the value others find so easily in themselves. I know Mom loved me and that she wanted me, but sometimes life can squeeze all that loving and wanting out of us. No one was to blame. It was the way things were back then.

I was born the fifth child. Early memories and events belong to my mother, older brother, and three older sisters. Of course, relatives and town records have certainly made their contributions to this journey of discovery. Having arrived at a time when years of marital tension, discord, and overwhelming hardship punctuated my family's life, I needed to understand the context into which I had been born. Recollections from others painted life's bigger picture, and this would eventually feed into who I thought I was and who I would become.

In the late 1920s, while the Depression took its toll, my father and his family were forced to relocate from Fall River, Massachusetts, to South Berwick, Maine. Due to the circumstances surrounding the economy, by twenty years old, William Lambert and his family had lost their farm, their home, everything. They were forced to live, temporarily, with relatives in nearby Somerset, Massachusetts, but, like everyone else, they also were barely able to make ends meet. My grandfather Edward heard there were opportunities farther north in Maine. He managed to convince the family that life would be easier in South Berwick and that they should make Maine their home.

South Berwick is a mere triangular tract of land near the southern tip of Maine. It is framed to the north by the towns of Berwick and North Berwick and to the east by the coastal resort town of Wells. The Elliot and York communities shore up the south end before reaching the Atlantic. Four ponds: Knight's, Cox's, Warren's, and Round, twenty-three bridges, many of which suture the town to its southern New Hampshire neighbors, also create its intricate social netting. With the boom of the shoe industry and its related businesses, the late nineteenth century was a prosperous time for South Berwick. When my father and his family arrived, the town, though financially hard-pressed, had several mills, shoe shops, tanneries, and small businesses as well as farming opportunities. The town was also famous as the home of author Sarah Orne Jewett and the prestigious Berwick Academy.

Despite its relative small size, South Berwick had industrial housing projects, some outlying farm houses, and a number of churches of various denominations whose steeples rose high above the classic three-storied New England homes. Among these, at the center of town, was St. Michael's Roman Catholic Church. In 1909, the Sisters of St. Joseph took charge of St. Michael's parochial school. My mother attended St. Michael's until she completed the eighth grade, and her children were to follow that legacy. A convent was also established, as well as an all-girls high school called St. Joseph's Academy. The Catholic Church, with its religious culture and rigid mores had, for years, blended with the town's Yankee mentality. Things were black or white, right or wrong. There was no place in their hearts for all of the gray areas which particularly belonged to life's hardships. There would come a time when the Church would play a significant, and at times painful, role in my mother's life.

My mother, Helen Marie St. Laurent, had remarkable resilience. She exuded a kind of buoyancy, a lightness that was grounded in bare-bones faith. Catholicism was the outer dressing, but the intrepid internal structure of that faith belonged only to her; she lived it. She loved to celebrate life and to accommodate others. She was a giving, compassionate, and warm person who never hesitated to welcome others into her home. But there was a part of her that looked the other way when things got too painful. "What will people think?" she would say. As children,

"Whatever happens at home, remains at home" was echoed to us many times. Her coping mechanisms made her a survivor; however, they were both her most blessed gift and her arch-nemesis, tightly wrapped together.

When I think about it, it may have been my mother's joy in the small things that first attracted my father to her. He was a gregarious sort of person, extremely personable and sociable. His friends considered him the life of the party, and he went out of his way to be generous and to help others. People loved him. In the summer of 1936, when he and my mother were married, she had no idea that his generosity was reserved only for others.

My mother was twenty and my father twenty-six when they married. The first two years before the children came along, according to her, were good. My mother worked in a shoe factory, and my father was self-employed as a molder. He had his own shop making concrete cement blocks. My father's family loved his new wife, and they remained in touch with her even after my father was no longer part of our lives. My mother's parents, however, felt differently about their new son-in-law. There was something about him they didn't like, and they tried to discourage my mother from marrying him. Dad possessed an abusive streak that surfaced only after they were married. When his temper flared, he was known, on occasion, to strike my mother. Even my father's family tried to protect her. On one occasion, when his sister-in-law was present during one of their arguments, Irene became keenly aware that he was gaining momentum and that his violent temper might well lead to an act of violence toward my mother. In an attempt to protect her sister, she stepped between them, never believing for a moment that she could be hit in the process, but she was. Her shock and disbelief were palpable when the blow fell on her instead of upon his intended victim. That's the way he was.

Soon after they were married, my father decided to build a house. While it was nothing fancy, both Mom and Dad worked on it feverishly, fueled by the dream of a home of their own. Her cut and splintered hands were painful evidence of the often back-breaking work. Her mother-in-law fretted, but Mom told her, "My hands will heal, but I'll have a home." But it was not to be. When the house was finally finished, my father unilaterally decided to give it to his parents because they didn't have a place of their own. My mother was allowed no say in the decision. It was how things were with them. Her role in their relationship was not important and, in his opinion, deserved no consideration.

In April of 1938, after the birth of my oldest brother, Bobby, things began to change. My father moved the family to a more rural section of South Berwick. As the babies came along, he embarked upon one business venture after another. As no one could resist his persuasive and charming personality, he could, and did, sell anything to anyone. He was also very adept at convincing people to lend him money, which often got him into trouble and once even landed him in jail. While getting the money was not a problem, repaying his creditors certainly was. He had lofty plans and "get-rich-quick" schemes, but his many ventures seemed doomed to fail.

My sisters, Carol, Claire, and Judy, came along with two miscarriages in between. During that time, my father built another home. Again, he did much of the work himself. The house was by no means elaborate, but, in time, creditors again knocked on the door and demanded payment for past-due bills. Mom was desperate; she knew nothing about any of these debts because Dad kept her in the dark about finances. They eventually lost the house, but that didn't stop him. He built a third one, and that too was lost shortly after I was born. Owned or rented, the homes were always far away from town, as if strategically planned to keep my mom isolated. With no car, no money, and five children, my mother was destined to a lonely and isolated existence. Occasionally, when she could get a ride, she would attend Sunday Mass at St. Michael's. These brief escapes meant everything to her. Years later, I recall her saying that my father wanted only to keep her "barefoot and pregnant," which, of course, was just another way of keeping her isolated. Of course, while she was embroiled in child care, my father was off on another "get-rich" scheme. She, like most women in those days, had little recourse.

My sister Judy was just fifteen months old at the time of my birth. Marital problems had been brewing for a number of years, and my father's abusive behavior had escalated. Worries about money and the need to provide the basic essentials for her children left Mom fearful and dependent. Prayer became her solace. She believed in God, simply and profoundly. Her faith in him and her love of her children sustained her through the chronic financial hardship, the emotional void of a negligent and absent husband, and the geographic isolation of rural Maine. And now there would be another mouth to feed, mine.

As my birth drew closer, my father spent more and

more time away from home. So desperate was the situation that it didn't surprise me to learn that on October 29, 1948, I came out feet first. Due to the traumatic birth, I was sickly for several months with intestinal problems requiring special formula. Soon after my birth, while my mother was in the hospital in a room with four other women, a nurse came in and asked, "Whose husband is William Lambert?" My mother said, "That's my husband, and Linda is my child." The woman lying in the next bed said, "William Lambert is also the father of my son." And so Mom found out that Dad was cheating on her. Adding insult to my mother's broken heart, a hospital bill for the other baby had already arrived in the mail when my mother and I arrived home from the hospital.

The internal conflict for my mother was immense. She was trapped in a small country home on Knight's Pond Road with four older children and a new baby. In addition to years of emotional and physical abuse, financial dependency had taken its toll. Most of all, she feared what other people would think. She dreaded the religious and social stigma attached to a divorced woman. It was the climate of the times, and she was a devout Catholic. The Church's position on divorce was clear; it was not an option. As interpreted, it was not only a grievous sin, but in those days the "sinner" was threatened with excommunication and banishment from all church functions and services. In 1948, divorced Catholics were not entitled to receive the sacraments, not allowed a Catholic funeral Mass, or to be buried in a Catholic cemetery. For my mother, there was no choice but to remain in a loveless and abusive marriage.

Several months after I was born, we lost the third

house my father had built. The house was in foreclosure, and we were evicted in the middle of winter. My father, who was still at home, uprooted the family one more time and moved us out of the South Berwick area to a small cottage in Wells Beach, Maine. He became less available than ever. While he readily gave money to charity, we were a constant reminder of how he had failed to provide for his wife and children. All of his dreams and elaborate ideas to become rich had been only mirages in a desert where there was no respite from the withering heat of the sun. For my mother, this move to Wells was pivotal.

The winter in Wells Beach was dreary and desolate. The howling wind off the ocean replaced the mild summer breeze and happy bustle of tourists and beachgoers. Thick, gray clouds cast a bleak spell over the dismal streets. Removed from family, friends, church, and familiar surroundings, the isolation for my mother became unbearable. The weather was cold and raw; there was no money and very little food. She didn't know how she would feed and care for all of us on her own. Her desperation and fragile state of mind convinced anyone with whom she spoke that she was ready to give up. Finally, the day arrived when she was convinced that the only escape from the pain and nightmare in which she found herself was to end the lives of her children and then to kill herself.

But, the next morning, something had changed. It was as if she had awakened from a bad dream. She thought, *My God, I need help. I can't do that!* She had five children she loved and who needed her. How could she ever have thought that she could go through with such a plan! She could not believe she had seriously considered ending all our lives. It was an option to which she would never return, but she knew she had to do something to remedy this seemingly hopeless situation. She had no idea when, or if, my father would return, but she intuitively did know that we would all die if we stayed in Wells. She needed to get us back to South Berwick, and make the decision to leave her husband. With help from family and friends, Mom took us back to South Berwick and finally divorced my father. The needs of her children far outweighed the condemnation of the Church and the community. She knew she could endure anything as long as she had her children at her side and, on some level, Mom knew she was blessed.

Family Photo
Back Row: Carol, Bobby
Front Row: Linda, Claire, Judy

My mother's courage was rooted in her faith in her church and in her belief in God. They were the core of her strength, her tenacity, and her ability to stand firm in the face of intense opposition. It's a good thing; she was going to need all of it and more.

When she could, she quietly attended Mass and often brought the older children with her. One Sunday morning, while sitting among her fellow parishioners with my brother and sisters and their classmates in the front rows, she listened acutely attentive as the priest prepared to deliver the homily. The church pews were filled, and the service seemed to proceed in that predictable fashion that made it so comforting. The priest walked across the sanctuary and slowly climbed into the pulpit. The people waited as he looked keenly over the congregation. When he found my mother, his expression changed dramatically. His face flushed as he glared at her over his spectacles. The silence was deafening. The pastor raised his arm and pointed his long, slim finger directly at my mother. "You don't belong here!" his voice boomed and reverberated throughout the sanctuary. "You are a divorced woman. In the eyes of the Church, you are living in mortal sin! You are excommunicated, and you are not part of this congregation. You are no longer welcome here." There was stunned silence; he paused and then added, "I want you to leave ... now!" My mother clutched her purse and hurriedly left the church looking at the floor in front of her as she blindly made her way out. She stopped going to church.

Mom never expressed anger toward the Church or the priest. The truth is, she rarely spoke of the incident, but when she did, her eyes would become filled with profound sadness, and her voice would tremble. "It was a terrible experience," she would say. "It was so humiliating." My mother later learned that the pastor had taken my brother and older sister out of class in order to speak with them about her. No one seems to remember exactly what he said, but it prompted my mom to remove my brother and sisters from St. Michael's and transfer them to public school. They were there only a short time before they pleaded with Mom to allow them to return to St. Michael's to be with their friends. She acceded.

As I grew up, I remember my mother as the most wonderful person in the world and felt very protective of her. With her bouncy, lighthearted personality, she did all she could to bring joy, love, and peace into our lives, and, in exchange, we canonized her. She celebrated life in a way that was contagious and that bound us to her with deep love and devotion for she had cared for and nurtured us through the most extreme hardship. She was a woman of indomitable faith in God, which she passed on to us in her words and in the way she lived every day of her life. As time passed, ironically her faith grew greater still, and this played a central role in the life of my family. We lived my mother's strengths through her until they became our own.

Personal recollections of my past would not surface for several years. Shortly after the divorce, Mom met Bob through mutual friends, and they were married within a year. They shared a codependence that, for my mother, suggested that there was a viable hope for stability. Although he earned only a modest living as an oil truck driver, Bob was dependable and able to hold down a job. This was Bob's first marriage, and, at first, he was kind to her and to us. My mother was incredulous that there could be a kind man willing to marry a divorced woman with five children. She did believe, however, that his drinking was really nothing to worry about, and at first it wasn't.

Chapter 2

The Farm House

> **Home is where the heart lives
> and the soul is born.**

For a very long time, memories of my childhood would be scarce and fragmented. However, with help from my family, the dense fog of unpleasant experiences began to surface. Burying them somewhere deep within me was preferable and easier than the prospect of recall. Recounting these terrible events meant often having to deal with excruciating emotional pain. When I was about two years old, we moved into Bob's small country farmhouse outside of town. There was lots of land, a large barn, animals, and a beautiful pine grove out back. Many of my memories are of delightful popcorn parties, birthday celebrations, and moments of the sheer joy of celebrating life with those we loved. My mother often gathered us together to enjoy what she dubbed our "night on the town." We sang songs, shared stories, told jokes, played games, and experienced the pure joy of laughter and spending time together.

However, there exists another part of me where the memories are painful, and I would rather not recall those. The events hurt terribly when they happened, and they seem to hurt yet more when they surfaced years later. The same wonderful home that taught me to laugh until my tummy hurt and the joy of family was also the home that taught me that life can be filled with pain and sorrow. We had no idea how bad it was going to get.

The farm house was a very simple two-story home with a tin roof that made beautiful music when it rained. There was a small foyer at the entrance where Mom hung our very own hooks so we could hang up our jackets as soon as we came in the door. To the left of the foyer there was a medium-sized kitchen that was painted a cheerful yellow. There was a wood stove, which was constantly in use, and a kitchen table and chairs. Attached to the kitchen was a small pantry. The aroma of cooking and baking that permeated the house was a reminder of the family that lived, worked, and was physically and emotionally nourished by its inner workings. The wood stove was also the only heat source in the house. The living room, painted purple and sparsely furnished with a simple couch, chairs, and end tables lay adjacent to the kitchen. Mom occasionally played the upright piano that stood in the corner, and we thought she was wonderful. Off the living room was a small bedroom where my mother and stepfather slept. Next to the entrance of their room were narrow wooden stairs that led to the second floor where the five of us slept. Later, there would be seven of us until my brother Bobby left home to get married when he was only eighteen years old. The upstairs had two unfinished bedrooms, one larger than the other, with a tiny closet in between. The closet was made of thin slats through which we could see into each other's rooms. There was no finished ceiling. Everything was open, exposing the sturdy beams supporting the roof.

We were very poor, but I never realized it, and it really didn't seem to matter. Because of Mom's enthusiasm for life, it never occurred to me that we had less than others. She lifted our spirits, making a joyous game out of simple things. There was no running water in the house, no electricity, and no toilet, so we used the outhouse by the side of the woodshed. About a year before we left the farm, electricity was installed, and we were able to have a television set and radio, which we thought was pretty exciting.

Bath time was the thrill and anticipation of Saturday evenings. Because we didn't have a regular bathtub, my mother heated huge pails of water and filled the makeshift tub, which was strategically placed near the hot wood stove. We'd take our turns bathing, and we were delighted. We found immeasurable pleasure in little things: jump ropes, marbles, and coloring books were treasured possessions. We thought we had it all.

During that time, my stepfather, Bob, was good to us. We had a roof over our heads and food on the table, which was certainly better than what we had before. During their first year together, my mother became pregnant with my sister, Cora. During the pregnancy, Bob's mother died. My stepfather took his mother's death very hard. He was very close to his mother and never really recovered from her loss. That's when things began to change at home.

Because of his inability to express his sorrow, an internal volcano welled inside of him. He often became very sad and quiet, and, at the other extreme, grew inexplicably angry and mean-tempered, especially when he drank. His desire to extinguish his grief with alcohol meant that, from one day to the next, (and especially on weekends) his mood and behavior were unpredictable. He still took care of us and provided for us, but things were very different.

While Bob was disappointed at not having a son when Cora was born, he liked the idea of naming her after his mother. He blamed Mom for not having produced a boy and made her life miserable. He was physically and verbally abusive, and the beatings were not limited to my mother. He also beat my older brother and sisters. I can only assume that, because we were little, he left Cora and me alone. Even at that tender age, my instincts told me that he liked me because he would smile at me or bounce me on his knee, but I found any warm feelings toward him quite difficult and unseemly in view of his treatment of the people I so desperately loved. As young as I was, I somehow wanted to protect them.

The peace and enjoyment of everyday life was often peppered with unhappiness and turmoil. We had fun when he wasn't there, but when he was around and had been drinking, there was enormous tension. We never knew what would set him off, which resulted in frequent outbursts of explosive violence.

One particular night, I recall awakening to a noisy commotion downstairs. I ran down in time to see him throwing my mother from one side of the room to the other. She had a bloody nose and a swollen eye. I ran to her, wrapped myself around her leg and screamed, "Daddy, don't hurt her! Don't hurt her!" That was my first conscious memory of trying to protect Mom. I was five years old.

We all went to St. Michael's parochial school. I loved school and enjoyed learning. I had good friends, and I especially loved the Sisters of St. Joseph. They took an interest in me, they were warm, and they laughed easily. If I talked about home at school, it was always about how much we loved each other and how much fun we had as a family. Most of that was true, but I didn't talk about the tension and fear.

Linda's First Communion

I don't know how I knew, but I was always cognizant of the fact that divorce was not acceptable in our community.

I wanted to defend and protect my mother, but I was also ashamed that she was divorced, so I told my friends that my father had died and my mother remarried. The people in South Berwick who went to St. Michael's Church were from Franco-American backgrounds, and were very closely knit. Family problems were not discussed outside of the home, and people were quick to judge. Even as a child, I was sensitive to people's feelings and quite intuitive. I desperately wanted to share with them what was happening at home but feared what I was sure would be rejection from my friends. I became an expert at hiding everything, especially my feelings of fear, tension, and betrayal.

The presence of my stepfather at home on weekends became ominous. I knew he would be drinking and what that might mean for Bobby and my older sisters but especially for my brother. My stepfather was terribly cruel to him, and the effects were devastating. For whatever the reason, Bobby was deathly afraid of chickens, and my stepfather knew this. One day, he grabbed one of the chickens from the coop and demanded that Bobby cut off its head. Apparently, the head wasn't completely cut off, and the chicken began running around hysterically. Finding this terribly funny, my stepfather caught the bloody chicken and ran after the terrorized Bobby.

During the times when my stepfather was working, I thought I was the happiest child in the world. I had my family, and that was all that mattered to me. I was able to compartmentalize the bad things in my life from the good ones. Without realizing it, I had learned to cope by being the family clown, and I would do anything to make everyone laugh. Instinctively, I wanted to break the terrible tension. I intuitively knew how people were feeling, and when those feelings turned ugly or fearful, I would do something comical. I'd bump into things, do some kind of crazy acrobatic move, tell a joke and forget the punch line, or just start singing. Everyone would laugh, and the tension would ease. I don't believe I was consciously aware that I was actually protecting myself from the pain of seeing those I loved unhappy, but I do know that I lived out of a place inside where I was able to separate bad from good. It became my mission to make people feel better by making them laugh. This pattern lasted well into my adult life.

Of course, we had animals on the farm, including a very nasty belligerent billy goat. I hated that goat, and he hated me. Whenever he got loose, he would chase me, butting my backside with his little horns. That goat chased me everywhere! Our driveway was about a quarter of a mile long but seemed longer as I ran, knees to chin, all the way down to the end, only to have to turn around and run all the way back because there was no escape. My tears of anger and humiliation only produced more gales of laughter from my sister Judy, who found the whole scene very comical. We also raised pigs, usually two at a time. We would feed them until they were nice and fat, and then they were slaughtered for food to get us through our long, cold New England winters. Inexplicably, one pig would somehow always escape and find great joy in chasing me. I still can't understand why my backside was so irresistible to farm animals!

Because we only had each other, we played a lot as a family, which ultimately served to create the unbreakable bond that held us together. Our playground was the open fields, the big barn out back, and the grove of pine trees behind that. We loved to play hide and seek, and I never could figure out why Judy, who was only a year older than I was, always found me. There was one time when I thought I would surely be successful in eluding the astute Judy.

There was a thick clump of woods near the side of the house that made a perfect hiding place. I climbed in there, sat on a tree stump, and waited for Judy to come by. I was wearing shorts that had little clasps at the end of each leg to make it snug around the thigh. It was a good thing. Had it not been for those shorts, the army of stinging red ants would have been crawling farther than over my legs and up my shirt! It turned out to be quite easy for Judy to find me that day; all she had to do was follow the screams.

On another occasion, I decided to go where no one had ever gone, and I mean no one. I decided to hide in the pigpen. Because of my size, the only way I could get in was to crawl on my belly through the feeder. It had a door with a hinge that swung shut. Well, that door turned out to be smaller that my childish judgment had calculated, and, before I realized what was happening, I was stuck. With my legs sticking out, I couldn't move forward or backward. Again, my hollering was so loud that in no time Judy found me.

While we all helped with the farm chores, we also enjoyed playing. Mom did much of the hard work, like milking the cow and tending the large vegetable garden, but we all took turns taking care of the animals. Bobby and my mother would chop wood, and we all helped stack it. After chores were done, we played jump rope, marbles, and roll the can, or we played on our tree swing. Rolling down the hill in a large barrel was one of our favorite activities, and in winter we loved sledding on that same hill using

Family Farm House
Back Row: L to R: Aunt Hazel, Carol, Bobby, Mom
Middle Row: Linda, Claire, Judy
Front Row: Cousin Sharon, Cora

large pieces of cardboard. We loved it, especially when my mom came out and joined us.

My stepfather's sister and aunt made Christmas time very special. If Aunt Dot and Aunt Hazel had not been there, I don't believe we would have had a Christmas at all. They loved my mom, and they loved us. These wonderful ladies filled our Christmas with special presents. Games, dolls, clothes, or sweet treats from them meant so much. Although my mother tried hard, she had barely enough to feed us, but whatever she did, we appreciated.

We lived in "hand me downs." Judy would get Claire's clothes, I would get Judy's, and Cora would get mine. Because Mom could sew, she made a lot of our clothes. When we started wearing petticoats, she'd starch them stiffly so that they fanned out beautifully under our home-made dresses. We thought we looked incredibly beautiful and elegant. On the rare occasions when we did get a new dress, we could barely contain ourselves. But, in spite of what others may have considered hardship, being poor never entered my mind. We loved each other very much and were happy with whatever came our way, and we were secure in our mother's love.

Life was quite normal on those days when my stepfather was away at work or out for the evening. On the nights he came home drunk, it was terrifying. Because of the terrible uncertainty of what was to come, I would panic when I heard the door creak open and then close. I never knew what was going to happen to my mother. The abuse and the beatings were not a nightly occurrence, but even one is sufficient to traumatize a small child for the rest of her life. When Bob was drunk, he would often go to bed with a knife and gun under his pillow, placing my mother in a constant state of fear for herself and for her children. During my entire childhood, I never had a sense of what a good, kind, and loving father could mean to his family. I always wanted one and somehow sensed that it was possible. After all, other kids seemed to enjoy having their fathers around. But the only father I knew frightened me, and, whatever scared me, I blocked out of my mind.

When Cora was about two years old, my mother became pregnant with my youngest brother, Charlie. As the baby grew inside her, I watched her get bigger and bigger as each week passed. She was huge. Our water came from an outdoor well, where the sun beat down and garden snakes came to bask and nap on the rocks. My mother was terrified of snakes, and to this day, so am I. My stepfather's idea of fun was to grab one of the snakes and chase my mother with it. She was so big she had trouble running. I'll never forget the horror on her face and her piercing screams. I ran to her, and as I clung to her leg, I screamed at him, "Don't do that to her! Stop it! Stop it!" Because of his own insecurity and feelings of worthlessness, frightening a defenseless woman, beating her and saying vicious things to her made him feel strong and in charge. Without alcohol, he was docile, but because he was so unpredictable, we lived in fear. We learned to survive, to cope and, above all, not to tell anyone.

When Charlie was ten months old, my mother underwent a hysterectomy. While there, she contracted a severe staphylococcal infection, which positioned her squarely at death's door. The doctors did not think she would survive, and Mom actually overheard them say, "This woman is all but dead." Later, we learned she made a promise to Mary, the Blessed Mother, that, if she survived to raise her children, she would light three candles in church every Sunday in her name. If Our Lady was not willing to negotiate, Mom prayed that her life not be prolonged. My mother was quite skilled at negotiating with our Blessed Mother and the saints, and she did survive the infection, but it took more than two months before she was fully recovered. Until the end of her life, my mother kept her weekly promise to Mary.

My stepfather stayed away from my mother while she was in the hospital. He couldn't cope with any kind of stress and rarely visited her. My oldest sisters, Carol and Claire, took care of the four of us during that difficult time. Our meals consisted of peanut butter and jelly sandwiches and canned chicken noodle soup. We ate it uncomplaining, but to this day, I don't like canned chicken noodle soup.

When my mother finally came home, she was weak and fragile but continued to work as hard as before. While we were at school, she milked the cows, brought in the wood, prepared the meals, and cleaned the house. She did whatever needed to be done. My stepfather did nothing to help. She often said, "Maybe if I sat back, it would be different." Mom did too much for the men in her life; she gave until she had nothing left to give. They never gave back.

One summer day when I was seven years old, a friend of my mother's came to visit. They sat at the kitchen table and talked over a cup of coffee as older women do. I happened to be in the house at the time and overheard my mother mention my name. I became instantly alert. My mother talked about my birth and how difficult the delivery was.

"I really hadn't planned on another pregnancy," she

said. "It was the wrong time. Things were so bad, and the last thing I wanted was another baby." I stood frozen on the spot. I couldn't breathe; I couldn't feel anything; I couldn't think. Hurting her or losing her love was unimaginable, and at that moment, something changed inside of me. I immediately decided that I would work harder than ever at being a good, perfect little girl. I would be so good that she would no longer regret having had me. I ran outside to play. I was the clown again, and I felt much better.

At only eighteen, Bobby left home to get married. He thought he was in love, but I think like many unhappy young people he simply wanted to escape the cruelty and abuse of his stepfather. He and his new wife lived across the river in Somersworth, New Hampshire, about six miles from the farm. I loved Bobby, and we all missed him. He was a natural comedian, like me. His facial expressions made me laugh like no one else's could. He had inherited his father's sociable character but, like my stepfather, he later developed a drinking problem that lasted for a number of years. This was very difficult and heart-wrenching for everyone who loved him. Today I know that if it had not been for Bobby and my sisters Carol and Claire, my mother would not have lived as long as she did. I know they helped her through a terrible time.

When Charlie, my youngest brother, was three or four years old, things finally seemed to fall apart. My mother changed. She wasn't bouncy or happy anymore, and she became lethargic and very depressed. At the time, we did not understand that she was having a nervous breakdown. Mom felt stuck in her situation and knew no way of resolving it. She seemed to have just given up, and, if someone did not intervene, I knew she was going to die. Bobby and my sisters also realized this and decided they had to rescue her or something terrible was sure to happen.

One day, when my stepfather was at work, Bobby and Carol came and took my mother and all of us away from the farm and that house. Without a stitch of clothing or anything else, we left. We went to Bobby's house in Somersworth, and it was then that my mother finally decided to divorce my stepfather. The lawyer advised her, "Because you left, whatever you want, you will have to go back to get. If you're caught, it's going to have to be returned." We were terrified. As children, we didn't understand what was going to happen. My mother and older siblings went back to the farm while my stepfather was at work. They quickly packed as much as they could take on a moment's notice, making sure everything was out before Bob came home. It was a frightening experience because, if my stepfather had been drinking and caught my mother removing things, the consequences would have been devastating.

Not long after that, I learned that my stepfather wanted custody of Cora and Charlie. They were his children, but I think he also wanted to take his revenge on my mother for leaving him. I was too young to know that they would stay with us, but I feared something might go wrong, and I couldn't bear the thought of losing my brother and sister. Until I was certain that they would remain with us, I again found myself in a constant emotional state of tension and worry.

We were safe in Bobby's home for a few weeks. It was the first time I had seen a shower, and it frightened me. When I was told, "Go in and take a shower," well, I didn't know how it worked. I turned the water on, and I thought the whole shower head was going to fall on me! It was also the first time we had a flush toilet, and I thought that must be the most wonderful invention. My mother spoke with some people and received help from the town of South Berwick, where we finally moved to a second-story apartment that was large enough for all of us.

Our life changed dramatically after this. At last, my mother came back to life. She gained back her energy and was again interested in life. Although she laughed easily, she worked as hard as ever. She made many repairs to the apartment, and we were very happy there. We could breathe without tension, and our nerves could rest. We no longer had to worry that my stepfather would come home drunk and abusive. Now that he was gone, we could simply enjoy our lives and each other. From that point on, my mother was a single parent and raised us by herself.

Divorce in our life and in our community spelled "different." The Church and parochial school teachers preached without exception that divorce was not acceptable. I often found myself defending my family when it seemed that people just didn't understand. Judgments were made, and Mom was often criticized. I recall the struggles I had with my friends when they realized I had a brother and sister with a different last name. They would say, "They're not your real brother and sister; they're only your half brother and sister." I couldn't believe what I was hearing! I knew they were my family, and there was nothing halfway about how much I loved them. Judgments like that cut deep and left scars. They made me feel isolated and alone, even with my closest friends.

After my mother divorced the second time, my birth

father came back into our lives. This was a pivotal event for me at nine years old, but I didn't really know what to think or how to feel about it. I was confused and looked for cues from my mother, who simply said, "Linda, this is your father. I will never stop him from seeing his children." He would come to our house, and he was welcomed. We spoke to him, and heard him speak. We saw him, and he us, and a father-daughter bond slowly grew. Mom, aware of this, allowed my sisters, brother, and me to get to know him better.

My father was five feet seven inches tall and weighed about two hundred pounds. He had brown eyes, black hair, a ready smile, a dimple in the middle of his chin just like my brother Bobby's, and I remember his brown baseball cap tilted capriciously to one side. People who knew my dad said I was the spitting image of him. He had remarried and was still living in South Berwick. Bobby, Carol, and Claire had visited him from time to time, but Judy and I had not seen him until the year he decided to visit us.

It took me a long time to trust this man and allow him into my life. He was my "father," but I wasn't sure what that meant exactly. Unlike my stepfather, his connection to me was genetic, and that seemed to make a difference somehow. I really didn't know who he was as a person or what our relationship should be. I did know that, because of this inexplicable sense of belonging, I yearned to spend time with him.

I remember once, as he held Judy and me on his lap, he told us, with tears in his eyes, how sorry he was for all that he had put us through. "I realize," he said, "what I lost when your mom left me, and I would love to have her back, but it's too late." He took a sad, deep breath and said again how sorry he was. For the first time, his demonstration of raw emotion touched my heart. Moved by it, I recall the first time I hugged my dad.

Judy and I both wanted more time with him, but instead he would give us each fifty cents and tell us to go buy candy or ice cream. At the time, two quarters was a lot of money, and we wanted that, but we also wanted his affection and attention. He seemed to find relating to us challenging, and so didn't really pay us a lot of attention. The others were older and were able to participate in grown-up conversations. He seemed more at ease with them, and I didn't want to interfere with that, so I had only rare, child-like exchanges with him. When he visited, I watched and remembered how he told stories and made jokes. In his efforts to make up for the bad times, he also did his best to listen to the others. He seemed genuinely sorry and sad for the things he had and hadn't done. The past couldn't be changed, but he tried as best he could to make amends by dividing his time between us and his other family, and that meant the world to us. None of us realized how little time we had left with him.

Chapter 3

Silent Questions

**Facing the unknown brings
strength in surprising ways.**

On December 12, 1958, having celebrated my tenth birthday at the end of October, I was to learn of the death of my father. My mother had asked me to stop at the grocery store on my way home from school. While waiting for the butcher to make up my package, I overheard two men talking about a William Lambert who had died. One man explained, "Yeah, Lambert and his son were trucking logs from the woods and heading for the saw mill. They never made it. Lambert was driving, had a heart attack, and fell over the steering wheel. His son managed to stop the truck." The other man raised his cap, scratched his head, readjusted his cap, and said, "Well, that's a damn shame." It never occurred to me that they were talking about my dad. I collected my package and headed for home. When I arrived, Bobby and my older sisters were crying inconsolably, and that's when I realized the William Lambert the men were talking about was my father and his son was Bobby. I was old enough to know that death meant my father was gone. I was too young to understand all of what was happening, but I knew that I'd never see him again. We had just found each other, and he was gone much too soon.

At the time of my father's death, the Church said he could not have a Catholic burial because he had divorced and remarried. I was in third grade, and I didn't understand why there would not be a funeral mass. In parochial school, whenever there was a death, the whole class would parade to church in order to support the family. My friends and classmates were not allowed to attend my father's funeral because it was not held in church. It was never talked about at school. My father's passing had evoked a predictable response from the Church, and my family, especially Mom, knew it could be no other way. I was confused and terribly hurt, but it would need to remain locked deep inside. I couldn't reveal how wrong and shameful it felt. The words were frozen in my throat, and my chest ached with the pain of unexpressed emotions.

It was on a bitter cold December 15 that my father was buried, and it was also my sister Claire's sixteenth birthday. It was painful for her, for all of us, even my mother. I recall seeing her red faced and teary eyed. I asked her, "Mom, why are you crying?" She said, "Linda, if it had not been for him, I would not have you." I immediately remembered the conversation I had overheard in our kitchen so many years ago. It was remarkable how that one simple sentence erased the ache of having heard my mother utter those private thoughts such a long time before. Despite her many hardships with him, she recognized and respected our loss and was able to move beyond the excruciating pain of the past. We were her deepest love as well as her lifeline, and my father had given her that. My mother's tenderness and compassion through the entire ordeal of the funeral will remain with me always. She had forgiven him for the bad times and was able to rise above the past, seeing the best in my father for the love of their children. Just as she had been able to differentiate between the pain and humiliation the Catholic Church had caused her from her limitless devotion and faith in God, she was able to separate my father's terrible behavior from the enormous gifts represented by each of her children. That quality in her always amazed me.

On the morning of the burial, even though the sun shone brightly, it was bone chillingly cold. I stood in the cemetery wearing white mittens and a hat, in disbelief that he was actually gone and that I would never see him again. As a child, all I knew was that this pain was worse than any injury I had ever sustained. However, my ten-year-old heart believed that, in spite of the response of the Church, my school, and the community, God loved me and nothing could diminish that fact. I knew that my father was in heaven. He loved life, and he lived with his pain in his own way, and, in the end, he was kind to us. It was certainly too late for a lot of things, but it hadn't been too late for his heart to touch ours. We all got a glimpse of what was good in him, and it stayed with us. If only he could have stayed longer.

Even at that tender age, much of my understanding of faith and religion and how they differ was shaped by this event. I came to understand that God's love and his presence is not limited by what we are taught by the Church and its officials. It is limited only by what we think of ourselves and our God. The Catholic Church and reigning public opinion dictated that, because my parents were divorced, they were bad people and somehow unworthy. I instinctively knew that God was bigger than whatever circumstances happened in life. God recognized the goodness in my mother and father, and that was all that mattered.

At a young age, I learned not to judge people or events only by what was visible because so often it did not represent the total reality of the situation. God often draws us to painful places in order to reveal to us his mercy and forgiveness, and to remind us that no one has the right to judge others except Him. I witnessed the institutional Church stand in judgment over issues in people's lives, and I came to understand the injustice of those judgments and the absence of compassion and mercy. I would not allow anything, not even the Church, to divert me from what I felt in my heart. Years later, when I joined a religious community, I learned that rules were often designed to be guidelines in our lives for the purpose of adding structure. Our minds learn the rules but also interpret them based on the reality of circumstances, observing, listening, and understanding with a loving heart.

My father's death automatically rectified my mother's political relationship with the Church. She was a widow, no longer a divorced woman and, therefore, allowed to participate in the ceremonial celebrations associated with the Catholic Mass. Her second marriage, performed by a justice of the peace and not in a Catholic Church, was never recognized by the Church as valid within its religious parameters and was, therefore, an act of living in sin. However, when my stepfather died in 1979, the Church welcomed her back into the fold. She was then able to receive the sacraments, and take part in all religious activities. I remember how much that meant to her. She was so happy, and we were happy for her. In spite of everything that had happened, Mom never turned away from her faith, and her living example had a profound impact on me as well as on my brothers and sisters. Because of her experience with the Church, my own faith was built on something inside of me and not on what the Church dictated was right or wrong. The policies of the Catholic Church had once decided that she was living in mortal sin because she was divorced and that she should be excommunicated. Subsequently, because she was widowed twice, she was then welcomed to return. Only her own true personal faith kept her steadfast, and, whether the Church condemned or accepted her, she never let go of that faith.

Our South Berwick apartment accommodated us for a few years, but my mother decided to move closer to my maternal grandmother in a section of town called The Landing. The area was comprised of several two-story duplex apartment houses built very close together. In contrast to our somewhat isolated life on the farm, our neighbors were now only an arm's reach away. Until she fell and broke her hip, my grandmother lived in a small house behind us, but when it became unsafe for her to live alone she came to live with us. I loved my "memere." A kind and gentle lady, she loved to crochet and knit, and I loved to sit with her and watch as she created delicate web-like doilies and warm mittens for her family, friends, and anyone in need.

Memere was very religious, and at times it seemed

her faith could move mountains. Whatever happened in her life, she always placed her fate in God's hands. I often walked by her room and saw her praying or reciting the rosary. Her expression was peaceful, reverent, and beautiful, and I know her simple, unwavering faith helped to fashion my own. My mother and grandmother were very close; they were friends and truly loved one another. Later, the experience of having witnessed their mutual understanding and deep respect served as a model for my own relationship with my mother.

Overall, people who lived at The Landing were friendly. While our backyard was a simple parking lot, we always managed to ferret out a spot to gather and play. By Mom's own design, our home was everyone's home. The pot was never too empty for friends to stop by and share a meal. Somehow, like the story of the loaves and fishes, there was always enough; the "multiplication" I used to call it. She would say, "We don't have much, but what we have we'll share," and we did. My friends loved the ease and comfort of our home and often told me how lucky they thought I was, and I agreed.

After graduation from St. Michael's, I attended St. Joseph's Academy, an all-girls high school led by the Sisters of St. Joseph. I loved cheerleading, dance, Glee Club, and many other activities. I enjoyed my friends, my studies, and my teachers. By then, my older sisters were married, and I babysat for my nieces and nephews most weekends throughout high school to earn extra money. When summer came, I always managed to get a job because, as a family, we had all learned that everyone had to pitch in to help. If I was not at school or work, I was generally at home helping my mother, and, in spite of the lack of a father figure, life at home had somewhat normalized, and the warm, loving surroundings as well as the peaceful life with my mother and grandmother had served to turn me into a real "homebody." We walked wherever we needed to go, but going beyond the town limits meant that we had to depend on others. I often found that somewhat difficult, and I felt restricted at being unable to travel outside of our immediate area or to go out with my friends. For a teenage girl with an insatiable desire to learn and explore, some days were just terrible. But my mother never complained, so I decided neither would I.

As I moved into my teens, the little girl who was once considered the family clown suddenly became tentative and insecure. I became shy and introspective and often imagined myself captive beneath a giant weeping willow tree where the draping boughs served as barriers inhibiting escape. My life seemed worthless and lacked purpose, and every day seemed strange and disconnected. The role of family clown was still mine, but beneath the laughter my life felt dry and bland. I loved my friends, but I felt that if they really knew me, they wouldn't love me. I knew my mother loved me, but I felt unworthy of that love, and accepting love was entirely too dangerous because of the risk of losing it. I knew I couldn't bear to lose anyone or anything else.

My need to protect my mother when I was younger changed to feelings of responsibility for her happiness as I matured. If she wanted me to help paint, run errands, or care for my grandmother, I would do it even if I had plans or wanted to do something else; I simply could not say no. When I did venture out to do something else, Mom had subtle ways of showing her disapproval. The silent treatment was the worst. On those occasions, I felt shunned; my head would throb with guilt at the mere thought that I had done something wrong. I desperately needed to be reassured that she was all right and not angry or disappointed in me. On the other hand, there were many good times. Just as my mother's relationship with Memere was close, she and I were also close. When I was fifteen, our conversations evolved, and Mom began to open up, talking about subjects we had never visited together. During those times, I felt wonderful and special, as though we were best friends. I loved her so much, but the enormity of the responsibility I felt for her also scared me. My mother was not perfect, but of course that fact was lost on me. I idolized her, and it would take many years before I realized that I had elevated her to a status to which no one could ever live up.

During my sophomore year in high school, tragedy again touched my family when my sister Claire and her husband, Bud, had a little boy whom they named Thomas. Their little daughter, Sandy, had been colicky and restless during her first year and rarely slept through the night. She and Bud were ecstatic with their brand-new little boy. Like Sandy, Tommy was also a colicky baby, and my sister accepted it with some philosophy. One night Claire got up to give Tommy his two a.m. feeding and stayed with him until he finally fell asleep. At 6 a.m., she looked in on him and was shocked to see the color drained from his face and discovered that he wasn't breathing. She screamed hysterically until Bud came running from the bathroom, looked at his precious, Tommy and ran for the phone. We all gathered, grief stricken, at their house. My little five-week-old nephew lay lifeless in his crib, a scene I'll never forget. We were in shock. Tommy was healthy one minute, and the next minute he was gone. Claire and Bud were in absolute anguish.

Tommy was in the house for a long time before the doctor and the coroner arrived to pronounce him a victim of crib death. Shortly after that, the funeral director came to take him away. He picked up Tommy to put him into a little box and, as he did, one of his booties fell off. That one small incident pierced our hearts with unspeakable grief and pain. Our shock at Tommy's unexpected short life made his death even more riveting. We were overwhelmed by the pain we felt for ourselves as well as for my sister and her husband, knowing that we would never come to know Tommy or be able to see him grow and live all of the dreams we had for him. It was an unrelenting tide of grief and disappointment as we thought of the unrealized dreams and expectations.

The three-day wake before the funeral was an eternity of despair. While most people were gentle and kind, a few made insensitive and thoughtless comments to Claire and Bud. I recall one person saying, "Well, Tommy was just five weeks old, so it mustn't be as hard as when you lose an older child. You know, you haven't had as much time with him." My sister and brother-in-law were left speechless. They loved that little boy no matter what his age, and recovering from his loss would take a very long time. Part of me has never recovered.

Why did such a wonderful and benevolent God permit so much pain and suffering? Nothing is more devastating or confusing than death, and it scared and haunted me. I was confused, and my many questions went unanswered. The seclusion and protection that my weeping willow tree provided only served to feed the insatiable hunger of my shyness. Even if there had been someone to talk to, it was impossible for my thoughts to arrange themselves logically into words. I only knew that the weeping willow tree that was my heart kept my thoughts and feelings camouflaged if not concealed inside.

My retreat into myself became more intense, and I continued to ask, "Is God not merciful? Does God care? Is God deaf? Does God know who I am?" The image of God as a loving Father was one to which I could no longer relate. Would God be like my own father and also leave me? God as a loving Mother was an idea with which I could more easily identify. I wanted God to be a "Her" and not a "Him." My mother, who was such a devout believer in God's limitless mercy and love, had taught me through her own example that I also should trust God; however, these questions came at a very tender time when I felt frightened and vulnerable. I was fighting to understand the meanings of life and death, and I desperately needed to understand how I figured in God's plan. I wanted to believe God cared, but I experienced him as a void and felt abandoned. I wrestled with my feelings, unsure of how to identify them. I struggled to say the right words, any words that would make me heard. I felt empty, insecure, lonely, and lost without a clear vision or a strong purpose. I felt alone and filled with an interminable sadness.

Life somehow beckoned me back, and, because I had become pretty adept at hiding my feelings by playing the clown, I was able to detach, automatically returning to the bubbly, lighthearted person I thought others at home and school expected me to be. Tommy's death was tucked away together with everything else hidden beneath the weeping willow tree that was my heart. My sophomore year in high school was hell, but I made it through by laughing and making others laugh. When they laughed it became easier to forget how I felt.

From time to time, during my junior and senior years, I went dancing on Saturday nights with a group of friends. "Teen Haven" was South Berwick's hot spot for teenagers, and it was a great place to dance and have a good time. Now and then I dated, but I really wasn't interested in any kind of steady relationship. I wanted more out of my life, and my biggest fear was getting trapped in South Berwick. I saved some money with the idea of possibly attending nursing school after graduation, but I wasn't really sure what I wanted to do. I was sure I didn't want to miss any opportunities by settling down too soon. I had already learned a serious lesson in that regard, and I knew that I wanted more from my life; I wanted something different.

I graduated in June 1967, and at the end of that month my grandmother died. It was particularly painful because I loved her so much and she had been such a presence in our home and in our lives. It was especially painful for Mom because she had not only lost her mother but had also lost her best friend. We were nearly all grown, and there was no longer anyone at home for my mother to nurture. She decided to return to work at the shoe factory where she had worked many years earlier.

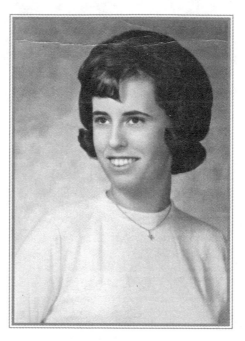

Linda's High School Graduation

Although we still didn't have a car, I was able to get out more and even got a job out of town. I commuted with friends and worked as a secretary at the Portsmouth Naval Shipyard. The question of what to do with my life left me increasingly ambivalent, but I knew I wanted to work with people and, for a while, considered nursing school. As the year progressed, something else moved quietly within me. At first it was a nudge, a whisper that became increasingly louder. The question was whether or not I had a religious vocation. I struggled with the question of whether or not God was really calling me, but at the same time, I was not ready to face growing up because it meant leaving home.

The nudge toward a religious vocation became more

and more pronounced, and I quite naturally considered the Sisters of St. Joseph. They lived what I wanted: to minister, to serve, and to be with people. I knew I didn't necessarily have to be a nun to help people, but that gentle push soon became a longing that begged to be fulfilled. Something was missing in my life. There was a huge void, but I was not at all certain if religious life would fill it. Above all, I wanted and needed to be sure. I was terrified of making a commitment to a life that might not be a good fit. I shared my concerns with my sister Judy, who said, "Linda, what you need to do is go and talk with someone and perhaps spend some time with the sisters." Of course I knew that I needed to do that, but for a bit longer, I decided to ignore my vocational calling. Part of me just wanted to go to work, continue to be the funny one, and ignore this turmoil inside of me, but that didn't last long.

One day I knew I had to climb down off of this fence of indecision. I called one of the sisters whom I had come to love dearly and asked if I could see her. I shared with her where I was in my life, and, as Judy had advised, she thought I needed to spend some time at the novitiate in Winslow, Maine.

The original novitiate was established in South Berwick in 1913 but had relocated to Auburn a year after I was born. As the community grew, so did the need for more ample space, and so one was built in Winslow in 1965. That October, as I entered my twentieth year, I went to Winslow for a weekend and found myself far from what was comfortable and familiar, wondering what I was doing there. I met the novices, the novice director, the Provincial, and several other sisters. They were very warm and gracious and walked me through the three-story building that overlooked several acres of land. On the ground floor there was a recreation room, boiler room, laundry, cafeteria, and kitchen. The second floor housed the novice classrooms, chapel, prayer room, library, another recreation room, and Provincial offices. Individual bedrooms and baths were located on the third floor. I learned that someone was hired to care for the grounds, but the sisters all participated in maintaining the building.

On the surface my visit went well, but not far beneath, my anxiety and uncertainty was palpable. Did God really want me there? Would I fit in with the sisters? No matter what the undertaking, I was accustomed to having high expectations of myself. I wanted to do things well without having to ask anyone for help or advice, placing the responsibility to do it perfectly squarely on my own shoulders. The question became "Can I really do this?" I returned home thinking, *I don't think this is where I want to be.* Yet the more I reflected on my weekend at the novitiate, the more I felt that I was being told that I needed to try. The extent of my ambivalence, however, was unnerving. I was reluctant to take the major step of telling my friends what I was considering, but my inner stirrings were driving me crazy. I needed to know if religious life was indeed where I belonged, but I thought, *if it turns out that this is not for me, then I'll move on with my life.*

I wrote to the novitiate and asked to be admitted. I had paperwork to fill out and tests to take, physical and psychological. Several weeks passed before I received my acceptance and was told that I could enter on February 2, 1969. As I prepared to leave home, I secretly wished we would have the worst snowstorm of the century. It would, I thought, be a sign from God saying, "Forget it, Linda." But, no chance; February 2nd dawned a beautiful, radiant, and glorious day. Was this the sign? Though family and friends were mostly very supportive, some gave me, at most, three weeks.

My oldest sister, Carol; her husband, David; and my mother drove me to Winslow, about 130 miles from home. The two-and-a-half-hour drive seemed interminable. I had said good-bye to all of my friends, my sisters and brothers, nieces, and nephews. I cherished my family, and leaving them was so very difficult. I had never been so far away from them, and I was going to this far-off place with much apprehension and uncertainty. I needed to let go and trust that my mother would be fine in my absence. I had spent so much of my life protecting her, so leaving her was painful and difficult, but the excitement and anticipation that something new and wonderful was about to happen seemed to push me from behind. This was also a way out of South Berwick. My ache and excitement were evenly matched, and they rode on either side of me all the way to Winslow.

The day I entered, I didn't even have a Bible or a rosary. It never occurred to me that those things might be considered "tools of the trade." I just wanted to serve people and be there for them. Odd as it may seem, I only came to understand, after the fact, what a significant part of religious life God was. That wasn't my focus. I simply wanted to be with a group of people with the same goals and the same thrust in life as I had. I chose the Sisters of St. Joseph because of the commonality of our aspirations and the resonance of their way of life. It was also safe. I was clear about that, but that's about all I knew.

In those days, when one entered the convent, you formally left behind family friends. Family visits were allowed only on specified occasions, and I seldom went home. My past was now hidden away, and my life was starting new as Sister Linda.

Chapter 4

New Beginning

> **The truth remains that life is a mystery.**

The late 1960s and early 1970s were as chaotic in religious life as they were in the rest of the country. Results of the Vatican II Council, which lasted from 1962 until 1965, were unfolding, and many changes were taking place in the Church. Religious communities were desperate to assimilate these changes, but it was like trying to hold water in your hands. Pope John XXIII had given Roman Catholic religious communities their marching orders. They needed to change, to expand their thinking and their ministry to more accurately reflect the changing times and needs in society. This was a huge and difficult stretch for religious communities, for some more than others. They were being asked to take a gigantic leap beyond everything that had been traditional and customary over the past hundred years and, in some cases, several centuries. This was more than a change in thinking; individually and collectively, it was a fundamental change in identity. There were no blueprints or road maps to follow.

For the congregation of the Sisters of St. Joseph (CSJ), the leap spanned more than three hundred years of evolving apostolic work. When the community was initiated in the 1640s, the sisters worked primarily in the southern and central regions of France. Unlike the isolated, contemplative lifestyles of their sister communities, CSJ was immersed from the onset in the trenches of humanity. They ventured into unknown neighborhoods and different districts of a city in an attempt to discover the needs of the poor. They then "set up shop" and began ministering by means of nursing, teaching, and orphanages. Following the French Revolution in the late 1700s, the Congregation established its Mother House in Lyon, France. From there, the community spread rapidly throughout Europe and later into Mexico, India, and, in the early 1900s, into the United States. The Sisters of St. Joseph were devoted to the service of the needy, no matter the year or century. Their philosophies were synchronized perfectly with my own, and their lifestyle, their involvement, and their spirit were what I wanted for myself. With a mandate from Vatican II and the same courage and enthusiasm for which they had been known, CSJ moved forward. Times were exciting and frightening on many levels.

In February of 1969, the community was transitioning through a myriad of upheavals and adjustments. It was as though an immense, historically rich castle were undergoing a complete modernization and renovation. The community administration had no other guidelines except the mandates of Vatican II, which, while general in nature, required serious changes, most of which required a considerable amount of guesswork and supposition, causing rigorous debate within the community. Some of the changes that were implemented worked for a time, others not at all, and the Provincial frequently found itself modifying its views. Cherished traditions and old ways walked uneasily beside innovation and untested approaches to community life. As fate would have it, during my first few weeks of religious life, I encountered both.

When I first entered the convent, a small prayer service was held for me as an acceptance into "postulancy," a nine-month period of adjustment. There were five young sisters ahead of me: three canonical, or first-year novices, and two second-year novices. Canonical year is a period of contemplation and religious study while a second year novice is more actively involved in the community. The end of novitiate training was observed by taking first vows. Final vows generally occurred five to nine years later. I took nine.

The novices still wore the habit, but with renewal it was decided that I would wear my regular clothes. I never thought much about what I wore until one day three of us were downtown and decided to go into a store. A woman saw us coming and opened the door for the novices who wore the habit. We all graciously smiled at her, but as I walked up behind the other novices, the woman released the door in my face. On another occasion, four of us were standing at an intersection. When we started to cross, traffic stopped to allow the novices in habits to get to the other side but restarted while I was still in the street. I had to run for it! The habit did something to people that had nothing to do with respect for the individual; this was a very sensitive point for me.

Several years later, in August of 1971, I received the habit when I took first vows. Shortly after, I went home for a visit. My family was very relaxed with each other, and conversation and humor flowed easily, but as soon as I entered wearing my gray habit and veil, a sudden inhibition descended upon everyone. They quietly sat there, looking at the floor or at one another, crossing and uncrossing their legs as they shifted in their seats. It made me so uncomfortable that I whipped off my veil and said, "Here I am! I haven't changed!" We laughed, but the power of the cloth, rather than me, had left its impression. It should have been the other way around.

At the time I entered, because religious life was changing so rapidly, the novice director wasn't entirely sure how to incorporate those changes into my training. After a few weeks, she extended to me a very unusual invitation. "Linda," she said, "would you like to work at our Mount St. Joseph nursing home as an aide?" The home was located about ten miles away in Waterville. I was thrilled and stunned. It was an opportunity to work with people, but it also meant I was the first sister ever to go out in ministry during her first year postulancy. I couldn't wait to start.

I worked at the nursing home for six months and, on my days off, took courses in prayer and religious life. It was a crazy schedule: seven days on, two days off, nine days on and four days off. Although I enjoyed my involvement at the nursing home, I found it difficult being the only postulant in novitiate. By nature, I preferred to be part of a group with whom I could exchange ideas and from whom I could learn. I really wanted to do well, but on my own, it was hard to tell how I was doing.

A couple of months into my job at the nursing home, I enrolled in a nurses' aide program at Seton Hospital in Waterville, Maine. My time was split between the nursing home, the novitiate, and the hospital. I was eager to begin working and living my dream of nursing; however, within a few weeks I received a big lesson about who I thought I was and what I thought I could do. Desire and earnestness do not guarantee success, and I learned very quickly that my plans to become a nurse might have been a mistake. I loved the work I was doing with the patients and the warm relationships I developed with them, but I had a very difficult time dealing with death, which frightened and confused me.

Becky, a fifteen-year-old girl who came to the hospital with a lump on her throat, was a sweetheart, and a bond soon developed. The surgeons operated on her, but tragically it was too late. The cancer had spread and Becky lived only a few months. The enormity of witnessing the end of such a short life left me feeling faint, choking back feelings of helplessness. I knew that, in many ways, I was emotionally impaired where death was concerned, and I was vaguely aware that my past might be the reason, but the recognition of this was only remotely present in my conscious thoughts. My skin felt clammy, and I knew that, without the presence of the wall, my knees would surely have buckled. "Oh, God," I repeated over and over, "I can't do this; I can't do this!" I was ashamed of myself for wanting only to help people who would survive. Both my past and my inability to discuss my emotions united to create a stubborn unwillingness to ask for help. Death evoked such feelings of powerlessness in me.

One after another, valuable lessons presented themselves, some small, others more powerful and relevant. One morning, I was told that there was a patient who needed to be bathed. The gentleman was in bed, and I simply asked, "Could you please slide your feet over and wash yourself. I'll be back shortly to wash your back." He calmly replied, "I don't have legs." Somehow we survived the bath, but I have never forgotten the experience. Initially I was angry that the nurses had not alerted me to the fact that the patient was an amputee, but the incident taught me to assume nothing. This lesson emerged often, and was quite valuable during my chaplaincy training. For the moment, my inexperience was an epiphany, but I gradually learned to extend my reach beyond my comfort zone, and soon my six months were over, as were my thoughts of becoming a nurse.

In August of 1969, the other novices were placed in various ministries, and the director thought it inadvisable that I remain alone in Winslow. I was sent to St. Joseph's Day Care Center in Auburn, where I worked as a teacher's aide with four-year-olds. Until then, I had not experienced the convent lifestyle, and I came to love my life there with eighteen other sisters. I enjoyed eating, working, praying with them, and seeing firsthand how community life worked. There was a wonderful vitality among the sisters that nourished our common goals. I was happy, but my contentment would soon be marred by two significant events.

I befriended a young sister who seemed somewhat troubled. After spending time with her talking and exchanging ideas, I realized that she was very troubled. One afternoon,

I found her lying on her bed, an empty bottle of aspirin lay on its side. "Sister," I said, pointing to the bottle, "did you take these?" She mumbled incoherently. I quickly went downstairs and found another sister in the house who was also a nurse. Thankfully, after lots of coffee and vomiting, she recovered but left the Congregation soon after. I was very shocked and confused by her behavior, and this confusion was compounded when shortly after two sisters whom I knew and cared for decided to leave the community. I was stunned, but I also felt hurt and scared. I tried to set these events aside, attempting to put them into some perspective as I pressed on in Auburn, where the experience was positive and everyone was very supportive. I seemed to thrive in group situations where tension was minimal, better enabling me to relax and put aside the heartaches of the past.

Gradually, God became a tangible and powerful reality in my life. The convent setting resonated with early memories of my mother and her philosophy of the importance of believing and trusting in God. She often said, "Without that, life is empty." God was always present in whatever we did as a family in much the same way that he was present in Auburn. This community of dedicated women served as the key that opened my relationship with God within religious life. I knew that God was the reason I was living there, and I also discovered while working in the daycare, how much I loved spending time working with children and their parents. I finally felt that education was where I belonged.

After six months in Auburn, I was transferred back to Winslow. Time was passing, and my superiors felt I needed to complete my novice training. Traditionally, a novice needed to remain physically in the novitiate for her canonical year; however, the community was in transition, and, as a novice, this affected me quite directly. The challenge of preparing me for religious life became more so because of renewal. Religious training was supposed to take place in groups and was not meant for learning alone. Five days a week, I took classes in Scripture, initiation to religious life, moral theology, vows, Christian life, and apostolic life. I joined a handful of sisters for Mass, spiritual practices, and assigned chores. The focus in novitiate was inner spiritual development, and my restless nature made frequent and numerous periods of prayer and quiet time considerably difficult. Quite honestly, I couldn't sit still. I was used to an active life where I was directly involved in ministering to other people. By nature, I was an extrovert, and I had a good rapport with the novices ahead of me, but they were on mission and only infrequently came back to Winslow. I often lamented to them, "I wish I wasn't alone…just to have someone to talk to." They were surprised and said, "Oh, Linda, you're so lucky to have one-on-one training with the novice director. I would have given anything to be in your place." I smiled and thought I didn't feel lucky at all and I would have gladly traded places with any one of them. Not having a peer group focused the intensity and loneliness of training squarely on me.

Part of my frustration came from the fact that I couldn't grasp the reasoning behind certain practices. Traditionally, everything was "in common," which meant that whatever you received from home or as a gift had to be shown to the novice director. If, for example, you were given a box of stationery and it became known that someone else needed stationery, it went to the needier person. As an adult, this is a difficult concept. I lived it, and I did my best to embrace it, but this common ownership seemed very strange to me. I understood that the purpose was to instill detachment and foster a diminishing appetite for material things. However, in my mind, the real purpose of poverty was to set us free, not to make us miserable. But, even though I was confused, I was committed, and there was never a thought of leaving.

On the surface, I remained cheerful and optimistic. I wanted to do everything right and follow all the rules. I desperately wanted to live my religious life as perfectly as I could, but inside I was fighting and rebelling. I couldn't control the happy image I projected any more than I could control my inner feelings. Life was an emotional roller coaster, but I was unaware that there was any other way to be except effervescent. My early days of isolation in Winslow were focused on survival. Concealing the conflict that raged inside seemed the only way to survive. At the time, I had no idea how debilitating this internal battle had become.

This was a time of great emotional pain within the community. While it was true that renewal opened many doors, the stretching and intellectual calisthenics that accompanied these changes produced innumerable aching hearts. There were many dynamic women of various ages who were willing to take risks, who forged ahead with new changes even though they were uncertain of their outcome. But perhaps the vow that was most tested was obedience. Dialogue replaced obedience, and sisters were able to express their preferences regarding where they wanted to go and how they wanted to serve. It was a revolutionary concept, and even more revolutionary was the fact that those in charge allowed it to happen. It took courage to trust the inner spirit to provide guidance and direction, but things couldn't change overnight.

In the past, the internal structure of religious life was built predominantly on the concept of obedience. One was sure one was doing God's will if one obeyed the superior. It was presumed that her judgment and voice were conduits for God's will, and, by willingly obeying her directives, we were not only doing God's will but cultivating the prized virtue of humility. The value was not in the allegiance to the superior but in the obedience to the spirit of God, which was working through her. Years ago, sisters and indeed most people who lived and operated within such a structured setting never questioned authority. They accepted what was offered and followed orders. The idea of thinking for oneself was not really an option, only because it was rarely ever done. A sister would never dream of questioning authority. She was obedient and therefore fulfilling God's plan for her.

Vatican II was a major force in moving religious communities toward a redefinition of obedience that inevitably unleashed a profound restructuring of religious life. Tremendous societal changes were also taking place, and people were seriously questioning what they had previously willingly accepted. Religious life was, in many ways, a reflection of the movement of the sixties to bring about profound changes that many found confusing and unsettling.

In the early 1970s, I was unable, or perhaps unwilling, to comprehend what all of these changes meant but was certainly able to internalize the painful tension and upheaval that was ripping through the congregation. Renewal brought unanticipated consequences to many communities. We no longer had to put our feelings and thoughts aside in the name of obedience, and during this time, many sisters left their communities—"mass exodus" we called it. Some of the sisters who left my congregation had taught me in high school and had had a significant impact on my vocation, while others I had met when I entered and had become quite fond of them. It was very difficult for all of us as we watched them leave. One day, when I shared my feelings with one of the sisters, she replied, "Linda, you have to remember that you didn't enter religious life for any one person. You entered for a reason. You need to keep your focus and not let your feelings discourage your own call." Her words helped me to survive many difficult moments when, one by one, I saw people I loved leave the community. Relationships were pivotal in my journey, in my life, and in my walk with God. Close friends were leaving, and it tore my heart out knowing that, not unlike death, their moving on meant that their new lives would change our relationships forever.

These disruptions shattered my security, but I believed that God had a hand in all of it. I knew where I needed to be; I felt I belonged, and I didn't want to leave. As I attempted to live my religious life as best I could, my journey continued, and I made every effort to understand what was happening. The months passed, and I was eager to make first vows; it meant my novitiate would be over. I could then go back into ministry and begin to live again. I was totally unaware that, as far as religious life was concerned, I was barely at the starting gate.

Chapter 5

Commitment

It is with faith that the heart speaks best.

My first vows were celebrated in a beautiful and reverent service that was held at the chapel in Winslow. I donned the habit of the community, which symbolized the spirit of poverty and simplicity I wanted to live. The year was 1971, and I was twenty-three years old, enthusiastic, and eager to begin in earnest the ministry on which my heart was set: education. I was given the assignment I truly wanted, and I returned to Auburn to teach kindergarten. In the building where I taught, I lived with several sisters. I felt like a young race horse who, after winter months spent indoors, was allowed to run in a vast open field. It was exhilarating and liberating.

Linda Receiving the Habit as a Sister of St. Joseph
L to R: Linda, Mom, Sister Laurette (novice director)

For the next three years, I learned how to be a teacher by the trial and error method. I loved the children and loved what I did, but I had a lot to learn about myself and teaching. The children often taught me lessons that I could never have learned in a classroom, filling the gaps in my inexperience. I remember my first day of school; I desperately wanted the children to love me, and I wanted their parents to like me. My personal perfectionism was at an all-time high. I had mapped out what I thought was the perfect lesson plan. However, by nine o'clock I had exhausted every game, song, and hiccup. To say I was panicked would be an understatement. In one hour, I had consumed every teaching strategy I knew, and the day-long program loomed large. *Now what am I going to do?* I thought. It was a day I shall never forget. The children did with me what they pleased that day and every day for the next month. Something was definitely wrong. If I was going to survive the ordeal, I had to learn how to develop structure, discipline, and some semblance of obedience I was too soft-hearted, too easy, and the children zoomed in on this like a duck on a pilgrimage to a soda cracker. Simply being a "nice" sister was not going to get the job done. These little creatures were the perfect homing devices for sensing vulnerability, but, with some time and several throbbing headaches, I learned to recognize the real teacher in me.

Gradually, I learned to successfully manage children with short attention spans and the rambunctiousness so typical in this age group while, at the same time drawing out those who seemed shy and withdrawn. Once I grabbed hold of the reins and gently pulled them in, the children were receptive and eager to learn, and my skills grew so that I eventually was able to reach even the slow learners and children with difficulties in other classrooms. There was something compelling in my teaching that eventually permeated all of my activities with the children. It was absolutely critical to me that every child be treated with respect and consistency as well as enthusiastic encouragement. I felt it was my responsibility to communicate to each child how very unique and special he or she was during every school day. After several months, the children were no longer unruly, and they developed the desire for and love of learning. They enjoyed coming to school, and I loved being with them. The parents, some of whom were disinterested at first, became as enthusiastic as their kids about the school program. I knew that education and working with young children was a good fit.

Community life in the small Auburn convent was even more challenging than the classroom. Unlike my experience prior to novitiate, a smaller group can't always absorb tensions between people as well as larger ones can. My reaction to tense situations continued to be lighthearted banter. Laughter was an all-consuming goal because it lifted me and others out of tough spots. I was "allergic" to any type of tension, whether I was directly involved or just a bystander. Being the "crack-up" was the best antidote to any and all unpleasantness. Even when I was younger, it wasn't anything I actually thought about; it was just something I did. I loved to play and laugh, and I wanted others to do the same. Sometimes it was appropriate, sometimes not. The problem was I couldn't tell the difference.

My routine for creating laughter always focused on the same target: me. My self-deprecation generally involved my very obvious overbite. Twenty-six years later, braces corrected a lifetime of insecurity. But for a quarter of a century, my "ivories" suffered the brunt of much derogatory humor by others, but mostly, the source of the ridicule came from me.

When I smiled, which was quite often, I was all teeth. Drinking from a glass or a cup became a musical event as my teeth bounced against the top of the container. Even utensils carried their own rhythm as my teeth connected with them while negotiating food to my mouth. Self-consciousness blended with my inclination to turn anything uncomfortable into a joke. Often, especially at mealtimes, I'd poke fun at myself and inadvertently encourage others to do the same. I gave no indication that my feelings were hurt when others made fun of my teeth. Instead, I laughed with them, adding comments of my own that further embellished the inappropriate humor. I imagined that, by making others laugh, even at my own expense, the ache inside would somehow disappear and, while I was on some level aware of this compulsion, I had to do it anyway. It had been a coping mechanism throughout my life for hiding the inner pain.

One of the sisters was extremely sensitive to what people said, did, or did not do. She was plagued by self-doubt and often compared herself to others whom she perceived to be more accomplished or successful. Conflict with others often arose because of her unpredictable moods. She could be happy one minute and sad and sullen the next. She and another of the sisters did not get along, and the tension in their relationship darkened the atmosphere in the house, so I automatically adopted the role of buffer between the two.

A state of chronic stress grew when this troubled sister sought me out for the purpose of quelling her depression and insecurity. My antics were an anti-depressant; I made her laugh. Simultaneously, however, her self-doubt perpetuated unconcealed jealousy and alarming self-pity. "Sister Linda," she'd say, "you're such a good teacher. Why can't I be as good a teacher as you are?"

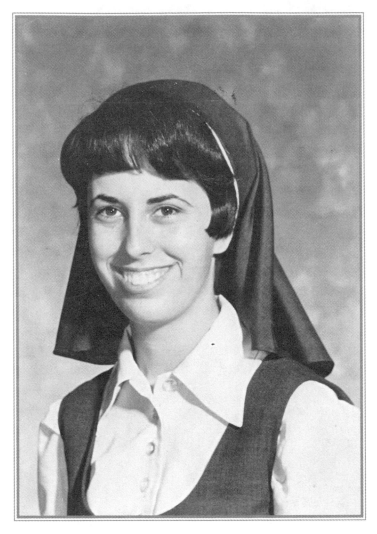

Linda Kindergarten Teacher

While my stomach turned in knots, I would make light of her comment and say, "Oh, that's not true! Of course you're a good teacher. I've seen you in the classroom, and I know you are." She did not seem to realize that the precursor to success is very often hard work.

One evening, while preparing dinner for the group, she commented, "You're a much better cook than I am. You're so creative with your meals."

I answered, "Now, Sister, you're just as good a cook as anyone in the house."

On another occasion, while preparing a prayer service in my room, she stopped to say, "You're a much better community person than I am. I wish I could be more like you."

In an exasperated attempt to distance myself from her and her self-pity, I replied, "Look here, Sister, you're fine just the way you are. The last thing you want to do is be more like me. Believe me, you don't!" As much as I tried to help her, I never could tell her what she wanted to hear.

Inwardly, I was tormented with my own ambivalence and insecurity and the ever-pressing need to be perfect in the community as well as in the classroom. Beneath the façade of doing things well, inwardly I was slipping and sliding, constantly unsure of myself and my behavior. While this sister was looking up to me for inspiration and new ideas, I tried to figure out what to do in my own life.

The problem was that, having come to her rescue as often as I had, I had, quite unintentionally, created a dependent relationship. I was her comic relief, and, as time went on, it was becoming an increasing emotional drain. I could make her laugh, but I couldn't make her change. I couldn't be responsible for her, but my insatiable desire to please made telling her impossible. If I said anything to upset her, I was sure she would hate me, and that would have been unbearable.

I managed to deal with this rather toxic relationship for over a year, but then my body rebelled, and I developed a major ulcer. My famous line, "All is fine," wasn't working anymore, and as hard as I tried, I could no longer hide the fact I was not at all fine. I was in constant pain. I couldn't keep food down. I lost weight and looked troubled. After finally seeking medical attention, Cream of Wheat and scrambled eggs became my staple diet for the remainder of that year. It amazed me how emotional pain could so easily manifest itself as physical pain. In addition the pain was even more difficult because, for the first time, I had to think about my own health and well-being. I was unaccustomed to this, and it meant I had to begin changing the lifelong habit of saying yes to everyone. For me, saying no was tantamount to swimming up Niagara Falls. As a result, my body mutinied, forcing me to pay attention to my own physical pain. This situation often reoccurred whenever I overextended myself. For the first time in my life, my body was forcing me to pay attention to myself. I was invited to move to another house. Under protests from the sisters, I agreed, knowing I needed a change.

I continued teaching for another year, and in the fall of 1975 I attended the University of Maine at Farmington. While taking evening and summer courses, I lived with four other sisters in Jay, Maine. I'd already accumulated nearly a year's worth of credit hours toward an associate degree in Early Childhood Education and I wanted to squeeze the rest of my requirements into one year, which turned out to be an all-out marathon. I was taking nineteen credit hours plus a practicum. I loved learning, did well in my classes, and had a good rapport with instructors and students.

Within my community I was actively involved in the Social Justice committee, which met monthly to study political and social issues. We wrote to Congressmen, Senators, and other officials while creating a community newsletter to keep sisters informed about regional and national issues we were working on.

Overall, it was a good year in the community, and the sisters and I got along well. We played a lot and laughed even more. I loved the lighthearted bantering and found myself doing things to perk up the atmosphere, whether it needed it or not. I teased and played jokes on the other sisters for the sole purpose of entertainment and the creation of a less stressful environment.

One evening, while at my post as dishwasher, I took my hand out of the dishwater and flicked my fingers at the sister who was drying the dishes. She reacted with surprise, and we laughed. I went back to washing and then did it again. After the third or fourth time, she said, "Okay, Linda, you've had it!" She grabbed a glassful of water and before I could get away, she unexpectedly poured it over my head. We collapsed, laughing uncontrollably. Whoever it was discovered that laughter increases the production of endorphins was absolutely correct; it was wonderful!

Shortly after the dishwater incident, another of the sisters, this one taller and stronger than I, did not consider my antics funny. Instead of playing along, she became increasingly irritated with every flick of dishwater. The more irritated she became, the more determined I got. After several sprinkles of dirty dishwater, she threw down her towel and said with tremendous force, "That's it, Linda. That's it!" I turned around, worried she'd leave, but clearly she had something else in mind. She suddenly picked me up more than a foot off the floor and sat me down in the sink full of dishwater. I will always remember the raucous laughter and the tears streaming down my face. It caused such a commotion in the house that I overheard a sister in the next room describe the unorthodox display in the kitchen with a certain undisguised resignation. "Oh, Linda is at it again, but she really got it this time. So-and-so plopped her in the sink!" I had reverted to my previous habit of "entertaining," which allowed me to steer clear of any real introspection.

I'd like to say I only infrequently engaged in my dishwater routine, but I'm afraid my antics were rarely measured. Whenever my focus was to entertain, I generally tipped the scale to excess. At the time, it was the only way I knew how to cope. I know I frustrated some and irritated others, but I never heard anyone say they didn't want to live with me because of it. To me, it meant that I fit, I belonged, and that was all that mattered.

In May of 1976, I left Farmington with my associate's degree in early childhood education. I returned to the day care center in Auburn overflowing with ideas for working with the children. Two teacher's aides and I worked very hard as a team, and I loved it. We had fun, and the children thrived in the loving and creative atmosphere we nurtured. At the end of the academic year in Auburn, I returned to college and became a full-time undergraduate student at the University of Maine in Gorham. The time for taking final vows was approaching, and I wanted to finish my education so I could focus my attention on preparing for the "big event." But I anguished at the prospect of the decision-making process and the inevitable questions that I knew would rise to challenge me. Was this life-long commitment to community really meant for me? Was I good enough? Did I really fit in? Was I doing the right thing? Did God really want me?

While at school in Gorham, I lived in an apartment with two other sisters who worked in nearby parishes. We were all very involved in our work, and our first year together was good; but things changed during the second year. There were unsettling changes everywhere.

At home, my twenty-year-old cousin, Donna, was diagnosed with an aggressive brain tumor. The sudden onset of the cancer left her family in shock, making it difficult for them to fully understand that she was dying. During this family crisis, I made numerous trips home; meanwhile, the sisters with whom I lived and whom I dearly loved moved on to other houses and ministries, and other sisters moved in. One of the sisters, a dear and respected close friend, left the community for a year's leave of absence. The loss was very difficult, but I knew the break offered her a window of relief much like an escape valve on a pressure cooker. A leave of absence was the community's way of supporting and working with a sister who didn't want to leave altogether but desperately needed a time out. More than the older sisters who had entered years before Vatican II, many of the younger sisters wrestled with their calling or unresolved family issues. Though I knew my friend would eventually return, her departure and absence was very troublesome for me. No matter how often it happened, I never got used to people leaving.

Residential disruptions as well as actual and pending loss made for an emotionally difficult year. I felt lifeless and lacked energy. Aside from immersing myself in schoolwork and periodic trips home, I tired easily and napped whenever I could. I thought my classes were the source of my fatigue, and it never occurred to me that there might be something physical causing it.

It wasn't laughter that kept me afloat that year, but prayer—personal and communal. At home, we met as a group in the evening to recite the "Office," the Prayer of the Church. Our weekly community meetings included a prayer service orchestrated by a different person each week. Over the years, I'd also developed a true need for personal prayer when, for an hour a day, I felt grounded and anchored. Changes and transitions swirled around me; prayer drew me to my center, that silent still point in the middle of a storm. It was the key to everything allowing me to step aside from the effects of my personal and community life. It was a way of recharging my heart and my determination to live religious life as perfectly as I could. In prayer I found respite, solace, but not necessarily peace.

My focus was to live the gospels, the words of Jesus, which carried so many layers of meaning and understanding. I gravitated to the Psalms, where David echoed my own distress calls to God. "My God, my God, why have You forsaken me?" he wrote, "Far from my deliverance are the words of my groaning. O my God, I cry out by day, and You do not answer; And by night, but I have no rest" (Psalm 22:1–2, NASB). I wanted so much to be happy, to connect with God and with others, but I had a deep gnawing feeling that something was missing in my life. My prayers were often in the form of supplications: "God, please help me to know what to do, how to be faithful, how to be the best sister I can." I felt that God was there for everyone else but not for me. Sometimes in painful exasperation, I'd look up and say, "You know, God, this isn't a *Sound of Music* experience!" At those times, I hoped God had a sense of humor.

I lived that second year by taking it one day at a time. One night, I prayed Psalm 63:1–2, "O God, you are my God whom I seek; for you my flesh pines and my soul thirsts like the earth, parched, lifeless, and without water" (NAB). I was feeling so alone that the words penetrated my heart right to the core. In desperation, I went to the prayer room and told God, "I need to feel your love. Something has got to happen. Please help me." I remained hopeful that something, anything, would happen. Suddenly, all those months of mechanical prayer fell like water down a fall. My whole being became filled with an intense love from God; I felt heat radiating through every pore. In those brief moments, I knew with certainty that God loved me and was present within my vulnerable, questioning self. It was what I needed to keep going.

I managed to complete my classes and, in June of 1979, graduated with honors with a bachelor of science degree in Early Childhood Education. I took a position for a year as a teacher at a Head Start Program located in the rural town of Jay. My involvement included going into the homes and working with the parents whose children were in our program. I was also in the classroom with preschool children, and I loved working with children and their parents. My health was restored, and my focus seemed deeper and more grounded. I was grateful because it was time to take a good look at my approaching final vows.

It took me longer than most, nine years, to make my

final vows. The delay was due in part to my own ambivalence, the time needed to complete my education, and to the radical changes in the community. Eleven years after my first day, it was still in flux. I knew I could teach; I knew I wanted to stay, but I was in transition too, and I was searching for clarity. Obedience and the overall direction of the community were core issues for me and the membership at large. Some of us wanted change, others were more hesitant, but the process of renewal was challenging for everyone.

With the end of Vatican II in 1966, the approach toward obedience had been completely restructured to include individual and collective consensus. Blind, unquestioning obedience was gone. In addition to open dialogue regarding placement, the community fostered the development of individual gifts among its members. Emphasis on individual growth, which began in the 1970s, was in full momentum by the time I prepared for my final vows in 1980. Once individual gifts were developed, the challenge for the community was how to use those gifts collectively to shape a unique and creative working presence in the world. Here was the painful spur in this ingenious plan: supporting the development of individual gifts gave rise to a strong sense of individualism and independence. The very qualities that nourished individual gifts inadvertently created problems for the fledgling blueprint of the community's larger picture. The question remained, "How do individual gifts fit into a common goal?" The difficulty lay in making the transition from independence to inter-dependence and inter-relatedness for the good of the whole. The Provincial Team and others struggled courageously for harmony and unity of purpose that we all wanted but seemed powerless to achieve.

I focused on trying to do the right thing. I needed to be certain that this was where God was calling me. It was the same ambivalent thread that had tied me in knots while debating whether or not to enter. I took everything so seriously and debated relentlessly with myself before saying yes. This desire for certainty replayed itself fifteen years later when I desperately struggled with the decision to leave the community.

As I prepared for final vows in August of 1980, I explored the breadth of my understanding and my promise to live out my commitment. I lived the vows of obedience, celibacy, and poverty as meaningfully and consciously as possible. These vows were not an end in themselves, rather a way to revere the spirit of commitment in myself and in others. I was committed to the Spirit in each vow as opposed to merely words written on a piece of paper.

I understood the vow of obedience as a sensitive and attentive listening to God, to others, and to myself. There was a threesome here. I would bring my issue before God in prayer and ask, "What do you want me to do?" If my inner self was agitated, saying, "I want to do this! I want to do this! This is what I want!" I knew then that this was "of Linda" and not "of God." But, if I sensed a peace and an acceptance, that was my cue that God was taking charge of the matter. I'd bring that discernment to an authority, talk about it, listen to what the leadership had to say, and then decide. Sometimes my decision was to do something I really didn't want, and by deciding to override my preference, I ministered as a sister of St. Joseph to the greater whole. Other times, my overall discernment led me to a different path from authority's preference. It was all about making a choice with the Spirit of God at its center.

Of all the vows, celibacy was one of the most difficult. I wanted to feel and be awake to everything I was giving and giving up. It was not a question of giving up my womanhood or my sexuality, but of making a conscious and willing choice of how I would live the expression of my love for others. As I matured in community, celibacy actually became more challenging and difficult. A sister once commented, "It gets easier as you get older."

I replied, "Honey, for me, it gets harder, not easier." I wanted to feel the loss, the absence of physical love, because I wanted to really experience what I was giving up. At the same time, I could love totally and unconditionally the people with whom I was working and to whom I was ministering. The two seemed to go hand in hand.

For me, the vow of poverty also held a unique twist. It was not about being "poor" but of accepting the beauty of all of God's gifts and appreciating them within a simple lifestyle. My community provided me with insurance, food, a roof over my head, a job, and a lifestyle I loved. My vow of poverty represented the effort to live each day in a spirit of gratitude and service to my neighbor with acceptance, judging actions and not people. It was being available to others and freely giving of my time, my resources, and my talents. Poverty was not a material issue for me and never was.

Of the three vows, obedience was also one of my greatest challenges. I was caught between my compulsion to be a perfect nun who followed through on everything as perfectly as I could and living as a dormant renegade who slowly awakened with each passing year in community. Most people did not know the rebellious side of my nature as I kept it well-concealed. I admittedly resented being told what to do as it somehow made me feel vulnerable. I pursued the role of being the perfect nun, determined to ensure continued membership.

Final vows marked the completion of a nine-year sojourn since my first vows as a sister of St. Joseph. God's grace and benevolence were never far from me or those around me. I meandered unknowingly, yet trustingly, through the various ministries offered in the community. Through those experiences, a maturation of my own faith took root. Living through pain and the loss of friends and family, as well as creative involvement, helped me to develop a measure of womanhood in religious life. None of it was easy. Through it all, the community supported my growing pains and my fledgling spirituality. Slowly I felt more grounded and aware of the reality of God's authentic presence within me and others. I shall never forget what being a sister of St. Joseph did for me, never.

Chapter 6

Turning Point

> **Who am I?**
>
> **Where am I going?**
>
> **What do I want?**

As often happens when approaching an important cross road in life, at the time of my final vows, I was also faced with some critical decision making regarding my ministry. I loved teaching, and I believed I was good at it, but, in time, I became increasingly drawn to children with a history of abuse. To pursue this professional avenue would have required returning to school for a master's degree in social work. I also desired to nurture my spirituality. How, and in what way, I did not know. I wasn't even sure whether an advanced degree in social work enabling me to work with abused children was what I wanted to do or where God was calling me. It made sense to get some hands-on experience before enrolling full-time into a master's program. There were no residential settings for children available in Maine, but there were in the Boston area.

I also had a personal reason for wanting to go to Boston. Two sisters who were close friends were living and going to school in Boston. They were considered a bit avant-garde, rebels with a propensity to try anything new and innovative. They gave the administration a headache from time to time, but to me they offered a daring excitement to which I was totally unaccustomed. They were living among the poor in a housing project, and I wanted to be there "in community" with them. Life in Maine represented boundaries and limits when what I really wanted, and needed, was to explore the world beyond those boundaries and to experience life in, what was to me, a larger and totally unexplored world. I petitioned the community to work in Boston with abused children for several months. With its blessing, I moved in August of 1980 and was hired as a house mother in a halfway home for boys. Here, reality hit me in the face in a way for which I was totally unprepared.

There were twenty-five boys in the house, ranging in age from ten to fifteen years old. They were children who, in their short lives, had lived through more abuse and trauma than anyone should see in a lifetime. Their stories broke my heart. One boy had been seriously abused by his stepfather, who had battered his head with a baseball bat. Several of the children came from homes where both parents were imprisoned, resulting in homelessness for their kids, and, in every case, they were very angry, bitter, hurt, and mistrustful of adults.

For many reasons, the boys had a hard time with women. As a soft-spoken, inexperienced new female staff member, I was a quick target for their aggression and projection of unresolved issues with the mother figures in their lives. While playing football with a group of boys on my very first day, I received my first black eye. One of the boys "accidentally" hit me in the eye, which entitled me to show up for work the next day wearing my very own black and blue badge of courage. It was only the beginning of my initiation into a very dark, bleak world.

Daytime was always filled with unpredictable tension and the threat of violent behavior. We never knew what would set them off. At nighttime, however, many of their defenses were lowered, and I found it to be a great opportunity for one-on-one conversation. Most of the boys couldn't handle physical contact during the day, even rebuffing a pat on the back. At bedtime, however, they allowed me to speak to them gently and encouragingly as I tucked them in, and I even sensed they looked forward to it. They yearned for the nurturing and warmth in much the same way a two-year-old would. But when morning came, again they were insecure and filled with rage. It didn't take long to realize that love was not enough to heal these boys. They required structure, discipline, and therapy. These were beyond my abilities. I managed to reach the younger children rather successfully, but the problems of the older boys were particularly challenging.

Michael was a handsome twelve-year-old who, under normal circumstances, would have been considered an articulate, charming, and intelligent boy with a rewarding and productive future ahead of him. He had a sweet face and a very endearing cowlick, which always made me smile. I worked closely with him, and I thought we were getting along quite well when one night something set him off. When I heard the commotion, I came upstairs to find him jumping up and down on his bed, cursing, and running through the halls causing mayhem and chaos among the other boys. I was alone on the floor but made my way to him. When Michael spotted me, he immediately ducked into a large cupboard with an iron door. As luck would have it, the door handle was on the inside rather than outside, something which I never understood. Michael had the door ajar enough for me to reach inside in an attempt to prevent it from closing shut. As I did, he purposely closed the door on my fingers. A sharp pain shot through my hand and up my arm. I tried to stay calm, repeating to him, "Michael, open the door. Open the door, Michael." When he refused, my eyes began to tear as the pressure from the door caused my fingers to turn dark blue. Out of desperation, I finally screamed, "Michael, *open the door!*" At last, after a few excruciating moments, he opened it, and I was able to quickly free my hand and call for help. Fortunately, my fingers were bruised but not broken. Sadly, I realized that love was not enough, and that I was clearly not where I belonged. I have often wondered about Michael: where he is, what he's doing, if he's happy. A friend once told me that, until years later, we often have no idea what things we have said to a child that might have made a difference. I pray that, perhaps at night, when Michael was receptive to quiet talk and nurturing, I said something that made a difference.

I was approaching three months on the job when it became evident that I needed a change. I hoped it would involve younger children, with whom I felt more capable. I learned of another children's center in Boston that had an opening in a daytime, early childhood environment.

This was an educational-therapeutic day care program that worked primarily with three-, four-, and five-year-old children who otherwise would be on the street. The position sounded ideal. There were about one hundred applicants for the job, so I was thrilled when the program manager called to let me know I had been chosen and that I would begin in three weeks. I immediately gave notice at the half-way home and whispered a prayer of gratitude to God for pointing me in the right direction. I soon learned that the right direction is not always easy to recognize.

A week into my three-week notice, the children's center called to let me know that funding for my position had fallen through and hiring was being put on hold. I panicked. I would be out of a job in two weeks, and I did not want to return to Maine. It was December, and I needed another job to carry me over until February. After a mad scramble, I found a temporary position at a local bank.

In mid-December, I made a weekend trip to Winslow with one of the sisters with whom I was living. In 1972, the novitiate had been moved to Lewiston, and the building in Winslow, aside from the Provincial offices, was converted into a Christian Life Center. Here people would come for retreats, counseling, and other enrichment and educational programs. As we drove up the driveway to the Provincial-ate, a heavy feeling came over me. I turned to the other sister and said, "Goodness, I don't think I will ever be able to come back here to live. It's just not where I'd want to be."

A few weeks later, I would regret those words. At Christmas time, one of the sisters returning home from a skiing trip was killed in a car accident. She had been administrator of the Christian Life Center, and her death was a tremendous loss to the community, both spiritually and professionally.

After the funeral, the Provincial asked to see me. She was both a spiritual as well as an administrative leader of the order, and I loved and respected her immensely. She asked if I would come to Winslow and serve as assistant administrator at the center. My first thought was, *Oh, God, not this!* This was not something I wanted, but a conversation I'd had with a sister before making final vows flashed into my mind. She had asked, "If the community ever needs you to render a service, would you accept?" I had replied, "Yes, of course I would." So, here I was faced with my own words. The seconds seemed like hours as the Provincial awaited my answer. I didn't have a job to speak of, and I knew I could render this service. I agreed to go back to Maine.

Painfully disappointed, I returned to Boston to pack my things, and, while there, I received a phone call from the children's center letting me know funds had been restored and I could begin work immediately. My heart was sinking as I replied, "I'm sorry, but..." I hung up the phone and thought how pivotal one moment can be when making a decision. I was disappointed and angry, but I also felt conflicted between the needs of the community and my own needs and desires, which were not yet clear even to me. I loved the community, and I wanted to help, but the thought of returning to life in central Maine made me feel ambivalent and apprehensive. I was just beginning to expand my wings in the city, and once in Winslow, I felt I'd have to tuck them in again. In hindsight, my life would have unfolded very differently if I had stayed in Boston. Confrontation with the reality of my life and how I was living it as a sister of St. Joseph, would have happened much sooner. As it was, part of me believed God had a hand in the unusual timing of these events and the experiences that were to follow.

My move to Winslow in January 1981 coincided with more painful changes. The sudden loss of the former administrator shocked the community to its core. Especially at the Provincialate, the sisters were grief-stricken for months. The Provincial Team, the group responsible for reorganizing the center, had no sooner repositioned people when, one by one, strategic people were leaving the community. The vocation director, a dear, sweet lady with tremendous insight and compassion, was the first to leave, followed a few months later by the formation director, a wonderful friend who was an inspiration to me and to everyone who came to her for counsel and advice. A number of other sisters left during and after this same time. We all suffered through these departures, and, to me, these losses were almost like deaths, each one with its corresponding period of mourning. No one could stop these traumatic upheavals. The Provincial Team worked hard to maintain the community's vision and fragile stability during the painful transitions, and they were somewhat successful.

Although I did not always agree, I had a lot of respect for this Provincial Team. In the years following Vatican II, their administrative and spiritual responsibilities on behalf of the community were extremely difficult and, at times, almost impossible. Three sisters, elected for a six-year term, made up the team. The position of Provincial, the team leader and spiritual head of the community, was full time while the other two positions were part time. The team was responsible for the fidelity of the province to its mission. They maintained a close working relationship with the Mother House in France and with our mission in Brazil. They met and worked with individuals and groups of sisters, helping to resolve problems and exploring new apostolic interests. They negotiated residential changes, requests for continuing education, and training for spiritual development. This team also worked with older sisters who wanted to slow down the changes brought on by renewal, as well as with younger sisters who thought the changes were not advancing quickly enough. Maintaining a balance between these two somewhat conflicting perceptions was a full-time endeavor.

Once in Winslow, I worked with Sister Agnes, who, in addition to being administrator of the center, was also part of the Provincial Team. The pressures of her dual responsibilities were great, and I wanted to help and support her in any way I could. She was an exceptionally intelligent and articulate woman, gifted with perception and clarity, especially in group situations. Her capacity for vision and understanding the dynamics of religious life in the throes of renewal were nothing short of sublime. I had seen her in action at numerous meetings where, in the midst of a heated debate, she would come out with an astute observation or a clarification of the issue that gave miraculous resolution to the conflict. I loved her dearly and had a profound respect and admiration for the quality of her mind and ability to focus. I became aware, however, of how the stresses of her responsibilities were affecting her personal relationship with others.

The Christian Life Center was an exceptionally busy

place. Groups were constantly coming and going. There were community-facilitated retreats, marriage encounter weekends, engagement workshops, cancer support groups, and other self-help groups continually in progress. Several churches and religious groups also rented space for their activities, and, as assistant administrator, my responsibilities were essentially to prepare meeting rooms and sleeping accommodations for groups coming in and clean up after they left. It was primarily a behind-the-scenes support position that I did reasonably well, but, much as I tried, my heart wasn't in it. I repeatedly had to talk myself into folding sheets and towels and doing the repetitive tasks, all the while assuring myself that I was doing something worthwhile. However, over time, it became increasingly difficult to "will" myself into the job. I carried on effectively but felt lifeless and purposeless.

Agnes and I kept the center running smoothly. Our skills managing the groups were complementary, and we worked well as a team. It felt comfortable and natural for me to move toward people, and I liked to engage and develop personal relationships through conversation. I loved putting people at ease, making them feel welcomed and at home. Agnes managed the business end, solved problems when they arose, and kept the center on course.

I admired Agnes's mind and her capacity for clarity and focus. She'd get right to the point and said what needed to be said, never mincing words. I think she appreciated my ability to get along with people in much the same way that I admired her organizational skills. There were seven other sisters who lived at the center, and from time to time there were minor conflicts. As a disinterested party, I found it easy to understand both sides. Agnes was direct and to the point, which could sometimes be misinterpreted. I looked up to her and admired her keen abilities, and I wanted others to appreciate her and see her the way I did. I was always concerned about her and wanted to relieve some of the pressure I was certain she must feel. I suppose it made me feel important to think I was taking care of her, whether she wanted me to or not. Little by little, I started to see glimpses of this lifelong obsession, and quite honestly, I was not happy with the view.

As a result of the enormous pressure and the responsibilities of her position, Agnes would sometimes retreat into pensive and quiet contemplation. It reminded me of my mother when she was angry or disappointed, and I found myself upset and anxious during those times. I'd be frantic to get even a trickle of conversation going. I felt compelled to try harder to be more cheerful, more helpful, and more agreeable. I foolishly believed I was responsible and therefore had some control over Agnes's demeanor. I have since realized that she just needed peace and quiet!

I recall one of the sisters telling me, "Linda, you're so unreal. You always talk 'pretty.' Everything is wonderful to you, even when it isn't. Get real!" The stinging words left me stunned. What could be wrong with seeing the brighter side of life? Isn't it better to be happy than sad? Isn't it better to give people hope? Of course, I didn't realize that she was interpreting my optimism as being disingenuous in the face of problems or conflict. The more I thought about it, the worse I felt. I didn't know how to be any other way, but I started ruminating. Maybe my best wasn't good enough; maybe I didn't really fit in; maybe ...

For quite a while, I continued my private little crusade on Agnes's behalf until I became vaguely aware that I couldn't do anymore. I thought my lifelessness was due to my job and the solution was to do something else. I hated to leave her. Part of me felt as if I were letting her down and abandoning my responsibilities. I often thought, *Maybe I just haven't tried hard enough.* But it was also clear to me that I needed a change. The truth of the matter was that I had abandoned my own well-being in order to help others, which is, of course, always a mistake. But, it would take another ten years for that realization to reveal itself.

I remained at the center for two years, and then in September of 1984, I went to Auburn to teach four-year-olds. In 1985, after being made program director at the daycare, I worked with parents and staff in developing and evaluating curriculum and designed a language program that taught the children the basics and readiness skills for reading. I enjoyed the challenge of the program, the interaction with adults, and I especially loved once again working with the children.

During the summer of 1985, four other sisters and I traveled to the community's Mother House in Lyon, France, to attend a month-long international session designed for younger professed sisters. The General Team leadership in France wanted us to experience the sacred grounds and holy origins of the community. We walked the same halls as our founder, Mother St. John, and prayed in her room. Through French translators we learned firsthand how she courageously rebuilt the community after the French Revolution. The focus was on renewal and recommitment of our individual and collective callings. I loved the diversity and individuality of so many sisters coming together from different countries. We were united under one goal, one spirit of ministry and dedication. It was a group experience I shall never forget.

Meetings, workshops, and pilgrimages to other cloisters and cathedrals, which I loved, were interspersed with periods of quiet and solitude, which further challenged me. Returning to the source, walking the community's sacred roots, and making it my own moved me in a powerful way. Throughout the month, and thereafter, echoes of the welcoming address reverberated in my thoughts. "Remember," the General Superior said, "no religious vocation is given once and for all. It unfolds gradually and is deepened at every stage of life." These words revitalized and reconfirmed the essential truth of my relationship with God and how that relationship was being expressed in my life and in this particular religious congregation.

As part of this amazing pilgrimage, we spent some time in the incredibly beautiful town of Lourdes in Southwest France. Between February 11 and July 16, 1858, the Virgin Mary appeared on eighteen separate occasions to a fourteen-year-old, illiterate, peasant girl named Bernadette Soubirous. Since that time, pilgrims from all over the world have prayed before the famous grotto with its healing spring waters. Outside the grotto, thousands upon thousands of people meander through or around hundreds of souvenir shops and commercial vendors who repeatedly call one over to buy this or that memento. Once inside the grotto, the silence and the reverence are so powerful that one is immediately drawn into prayer.

I sat in front of the grotto for hours watching an uninterrupted procession. Travelers of every nationality, parents wheeling their crippled children, and older children carting their maimed or deformed parents paused before the statue of Mary. That day I saw hundreds of people in emotional and physical pain walk into this holy place only to leave with a quiet expression of peace and joy for having touched the sanctified ground of Lourdes. That day, I learned that a healing of the spirit was as miraculous as a healing of the body. There are many ceremonies each day at Lourdes, but the most moving is the candlelit procession of the rosary held every night at eight thirty. The Hail Mary is prayed aloud in many different languages, but the reverence and individual candle flames of thousands merge into beautiful unity that transcends all differences in race, religion, and culture. That night, I united with Mary in a most profound way. My heart told her, "I know you will be with me whatever I have to go through; I know you will be there." At that moment, I could not have known how very much I would need her in my life and the losses that were ahead of me.

I returned to Auburn in time for the school year, feeling my spirit re-energized, God became a more vital, living presence in my consciousness. On another level, I felt that my time in education was running out. I had given a number of years to teaching, but now I yearned to move more deeply into a period of self-discovery, though I was not sure in what direction it would take me.

Earlier that summer I'd attended a workshop given by Matthew Fox, a Dominican priest, who shared his vision and commitment to what he called "creation spirituality." Fox described his "Institute in Culture and Creation Spirituality" (ICCS), founded in 1976 at Holy Name College in

Oakland, California. ICCS offered a nine-month intensive master's program, and the concept offered an earthiness to values and ideals that I found very attractive. My summer in France only increased my desire to attend. From what I knew, I believed Fox's program would strengthen and solidify the spirituality I felt. I remained as program director while also exploring the possibility of enrolling at ICCS. Suddenly all plans came to a halt.

I had been having terrible problems with my menstrual cycle and was hospitalized on several occasions to have a D&C, a laparoscopy, and recurring cysts removed. I was told I did not ovulate because benign cysts kept forming on my ovaries. No sooner were they removed than they returned twice their original size. I was losing weight and menstruating thirty out of thirty-one days. Due to the stress on my immune system, I was prone to colds and infections. Before long, I came down with what I thought was strep throat.

The doctor informed me, "You don't have strep throat, Linda. You have tonsillitis. I know you've had your tonsils removed, but the infection is located right where your tonsils were." The doctor paused for a moment and looked directly at me. I could tell he was trying to tell me something I didn't want to hear. He said, "Look, Linda, you need to make a decision. Either you have a hysterectomy and go on hormone replacement therapy, or you continue having surgery to have the cysts removed. It's your choice, but I would recommend the hysterectomy."

Because of my weakened state, repeated surgeries were no longer an option. I knew the doctor was right, but I felt a dull, aching fear whenever the word hysterectomy was mentioned. After confirming the diagnosis with a second opinion, surgery was finally scheduled for April of 1986. I was thirty-eight years old, the same age my mother was when she had her hysterectomy. Prior to surgery, I was an emotional wreck. Fear floated on top of my impending loss like oil on water. My mind understood the medical necessity for the operation, but my heart and my body rebelled with a heated rage of having to be mutilated in order to heal. My reaction confused some of the women whom I sought out for support. Several echoed a similar refrain, such as, "Oh, I wish I were going through that so I wouldn't have my period every month." Another woman who'd had a hysterectomy casually said, "Nothing to worry about. It's a piece of cake." I wanted to scream, but instead I walked away overwhelmed and frustrated for not being able to communicate how I really felt.

I was terrified of the loss. I hated the fact that the part of my body that carried the potential for life was going to be carved out of me permanently. Even though I had been a sister for eighteen years, I cherished my body's potential ability to create life. I feared the loss of control over my body and how it would react after surgery. Would I get fat, grow old sooner, and have hot flashes? All of the information and intelligent conversation in the world could not alleviate my anxiety and fear. I was losing something I couldn't see, but emotionally I was very much in touch with what it meant. I have since learned that my fears and terrors were not unlike many other women in a similar situation, but, in those days, there was little real conversation about such personal matters.

Fortunately, the hysterectomy was partial; the uterus was removed, and the ovaries were left intact. That meant menopause would not be abrupt, and I would not need long-term estrogen replacement therapy. I remember touching the scar and being aware of emptiness, a feeling of powerlessness, and a sense that something holy had been removed from my body. Integrating the emotional, spiritual, and psychological repercussions of the surgery took much longer than I would have imagined possible.

I am aware that not all women face the same fears when confronted with this kind of surgery. I am also aware that all the preparation in the world does not eliminate the need for going through the stages of loss, many of which are triggered by the surgery itself. The intensity of my reaction would have happened regardless of whether I was in community, married, or single, and although the operation brought relief to a serious medical situation, a hysterectomy meant losing part of me. Ordinarily, my response would have been to bypass the emotional pain, but this time I found that impossible.

Talking through my fears was life saving, facing the issue of loss was very important, and being affirmed as a woman was critical. A few women attempted to console me with a philosophical approach. "Now you can give birth to other kinds of things." Unfortunately, that did not resonate for me. My close friends, however, allowed me to be worried about being a woman first and religious second. They knew better than to simply advise me to go and pray to overcome my pain. Several women, both in and out of the community, who had had hysterectomies were exceptionally sensitive. They understood the anguish I felt and allowed me to express it as best as I could. With them, I fully experienced the depth and empathy of women ministering to women. Through these friends, the feminine aspect of God's presence became clearly visible, and it was both beautiful and healing.

As spring turned to summer, my body and spirit gradually healed. During my recuperation, I continued to explore the possibility of enrolling in Matthew Fox's creation spirituality program. Something in me wanted and needed to be there. The community, however, held a different position, which I could certainly understand. Matthew Fox was a rather controversial figure, and more conservative groups preferred to keep their distance from his programs. As it turned out, plans for heading west would be abruptly postponed. More shattering losses lay ahead.

Chapter 7

Heart Disruptions

> **Our experience of death is
> one of separation—a tearing apart
> and the hope for wholeness once again.**

My brother Bobby was not only a devoted husband and brother, but he thoroughly and completely adored his son, Timmy. Between 1982 and 1986, Bobby suffered two heart attacks, and his health was delicate, but that never stopped him.

I recall a conversation I had with Bobby back in February, a few months before my surgery. He was in the hospital for a second heart attack, and I needed to see him and be there for him. That day, Bobby talked to me in a way that clearly told me who he was.

As I walked into his hospital room, I said, "Bobby, how are you?"

He started talking, and I did not open my mouth once (a miracle in its own right!) "Linda," he said, "I don't want

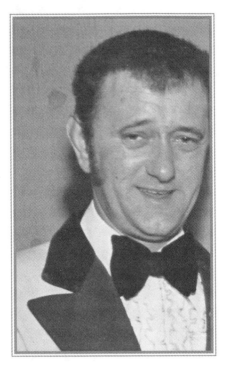

My brother Bob

to die. I'm forty-seven years old, and I've done a lot in my life. I'm not afraid of dying, but the hardest thing about it is leaving people here. I want to see Timmy graduate from grammar school. I'd like to see him graduate from college, but I don't think that's going to happen." He paused a long time, then said, "I just look at my life so differently now."

Bobby valued his life, and he now seemed to be looking at where it was taking him. He seemed aware that many of the people he had once loved that had died would be waiting for him in the next life. He talked about our father, our "memere," and others. Then he said, "Linda, I'm going to miss you. I'm going to miss Dee [his wife], I'm going to miss Mom, and … and …" He named us all. This was a side of him I had not known. He was always making jokes, and I had seldom seen him serious about anything, but here he was talking about his life and death, what he loved and didn't love.

Bobby was very different from the rest of the family. After he left home, he was often in trouble. He drank a great deal and was jailed several times because of wrong choices. My mother always worried about him, and it pained her deeply to see how his life was going, or not going. It now seemed as though he saw himself completely removed from all of that turmoil.

Beginning with his first heart attack four years earlier, I came to know Bobby as I'd never known him. He was completely open and totally clear. By nature, he was a meticulously organized man. His previous heart attack had changed his life dramatically and brought him closer to his family, his wife, and Timmy. With this attack, he was struggling with the deeper meaning of his existence. He struggled with purpose and other hard issues. "I'm not afraid of dying," he said again, "but why do I have to die so young?" One of his greatest desires was to live life fully until his final moment. "I want to live until I die," he said. "I've had a chance to look at my life, and I want to savor each moment I can."

It was July 14th, 1986, and Bobby was at a father-son baseball game with thirteen-year-old Timmy. Because he was not at all well, he was in the bleachers, this time choosing to sit out the game. The team was minus one dad, so they asked him if he would pinch hit. In hindsight, he should not have stepped up to the plate.

Bobby felt the need to do this for himself and for Timmy. He got up to bat, connected with the ball, and to everyone's surprise, he hit a home run. The crowd rose to its feet and hollered encouragement. Bobby ran the bases as the people in the stands cheered as though they were in the tenth inning of the World Series, but when he arrived at home plate, he collapsed. Amidst the shock and commotion, Timmy ran to his dad to try to wake him. Bobby never regained consciousness. While waiting for help, people were milling around in disbelief, hovering over him. The ambulance arrived, but Bobby died on the way to the hospital.

When I received the phone call telling me that Bobby had died, the shock mobilized me to pull myself together physically and emotionally. I wanted to be fully present for his family as well as for my mother and my family. There was no time for me to grieve. I felt people needed me to be strong and in control, so I got busy seeing to the many details: the liturgy, the service, and being supportive for others. A few weeks later at a seven-day retreat in East Gloucester, Massachusetts, I finally realized my brother was gone.

It didn't come all at once but in waves like an incoming tide that overwhelmed me with emotional pain. Death was dark, lonely, and final. The sadness I felt seemed to bore into the core of my being. When the tears finally came, I cried for everyone and everything. I cried for Bobby, for his years with alcohol, and for past events that drove him to it. I cried for my family, my mother and her trials, my father, and the sisters I cherished who'd left community. I cried for myself. I was flooded with a sea of memories and emotions, and in the center of it was Bobby. He was the crystal clear "eye" in the middle of a terrifying storm.

On that seven-day retreat, I often played and re-played the scene of Bobby running the bases as I imagined it. I'm sure he must have experienced some pressure, some pain in his chest, but he continued running until he made it to home plate. The whole scene of running, coming in to home plate, and dying, seemed so significant. Bobby died the way he wanted to: awake, moving, and engaged in life. In my heart, I know that God was at home plate waiting for him, and I know that Timmy will never forget his dad running for him ... for both of them.

There was a generational thread in the deaths in my family that was more than coincidence. When my father died, Bobby was with him; when Bobby died, Timmy was with him. My father and Bobby were both forty-eight when their hearts beat for the last time. They were able to face the dark side of their lives before they died, realizing at last what was really important. Bobby seemed to know it was coming. He had experienced his first heart attack when he was forty-four, shortly after the sudden death of his eighteen-year-old son from a previous marriage, who was killed in a motorcycle accident. Bobby's second attack came three and a half years later. His third one was fatal. Bobby taught me that dying was not separate from living but an integral part of the process. The memory of my brother's life and him sharing with me touched me as a point of grace. He will always be with me.

The long summer ended, and the crisp smell of fall was in the air as the Maine foliage neared the end of its colorful radiance. I remember marveling at the fragrance of the changing seasons, the dance of falling leaves. Death and loss had been such a large part of the previous months, and

I was trying to grasp the pain and darkness as though it were a mass I could hold firmly in my hand, something tangible and concrete. I welcomed the fall as a reflection of what I was living.

Once again, I approached the community with my desire to go to California and attend Matthew Fox's institute. The Provincial Team was very reticent and preferred that I not involve myself in Fox's creation spirituality program. I persisted, and continued to write one letter after another. Finally in October, I received a favorable response, and the blessing to apply for the following year. I was ecstatic. I called my mother to tell her the good news, and she was thrilled for me.

By the start of November, the day care center in Auburn was in full swing. On November 3, I had had a tough day and was in my room praying while some of the sisters were preparing dinner. At five fifteen, someone in the house came to tell me my sister Carol was on the phone. As though propelled by another force, I walked deliberately to the telephone, said hello, and Carol answered simply, "Linda, Mom's gone."

Not grasping what she was trying to say, I asked, "Well, where did she go?"

She said, again, "Linda, Mom's gone." By the second time I understood, but I was in disbelief. I was still grieving for my brother Bobby; this could not be happening. My whole being fell into a state of shock... not my Mom! I kept thinking, *Oh, God, it can't be true. It's too fast! It's too sudden!* She was my mom, my dad, and my best friend, and now she was being taken from me! Nothing could control the devastating and overwhelming grief and sorrow.

Inconsolable, I leaned against the wall and then collapsed, sliding all the way down. I couldn't scream loud enough. My whole body ached. I was not in control. A deep, dark void encircled my body, and I just screamed. The sisters helped me. Someone grabbed the phone while the others got on the floor with me. They just held me. Over and over, I repeated, "No! No! No! No!" as if by uttering the word *no* I could somehow change what had happened. My world fell out from under me, and I was lost in pain. My body ached and felt cold. Denial swept over me, and I hoped this was just a bad dream from which I'd awaken, the pain and void disappearing in the dawn. But it wasn't a dream.

Two sisters drove me to my mother's home that night. The next three days were some of the most difficult of my life. Understandably, my family was in shock, and we were all coping the best way we could, taking care of arrangements and making funeral plans, but it was very, very hard. When I first arrived at my mother's house, we decided that I should stay there for the next several days with my sister Cora, who also lived out of town. On the second night, Cora said to me, "Linda, I really can't stay here. It's just too hard to be here without Mom. Why don't we stay at Claire and Bud's house?" I thought for a moment but said, "I can't. I need to stay here. If you need to go, you go. I have to stay here. This home, my home, is going to be closed, and I want to spend as much time here as I can. I need to be as near as I can to Mom." Cora understood. "No," she said, "I'm not going to leave." We stayed together all three nights, and then we went to my sister Claire's home.

I learned that my mother had died on November 2 from

what appeared to be congestive heart failure. Evidently, it was very quick. My sister talked with her in the morning, and everything seemed fine. On Sunday evenings, my aunt and her daughter customarily went to my mother's house to play cards. It was a Sunday evening ritual. My mother baked something during the day, cookies or some sweets, and they spent the evening playing cards and enjoying each other. Everyone in the family knew of this Sunday-night routine and visited earlier in the day to avoid interrupting their cherished time.

She died sometime between two and four o'clock on Sunday afternoon. The TV was on. It looked as if she had been lying on the couch. She probably experienced some discomfort, got up quickly, and fell, dying instantly. That evening my aunt called my mother to arrange for the card game and, when there was no answer, thought my mother must be out. My aunt and my cousin drove by the house, saw that there were no lights on, and thought my mother was at one of my sisters' or my younger brother's house. On Monday, November 3, my sister Carol stopped by after work to have a cup of coffee with my mother. She knocked on the door, found it unlocked, heard the TV, and said, "Hi, Mom," but there was no answer. She walked through the kitchen to the living room, looked over, and saw my mother on the floor. Carol immediately went over and moved the coffee table out of the way. It had toppled over when she fell. Carol tried to shake her. She said she knew my mother was dead but didn't want to believe it. She got up, walked around, came back, and tried to shake my mother again. Then she knew. She called 911 and then her daughter, Patty. It was not long before people began to arrive. The police came and interrogated Carol because she had moved my mother. Then my other sisters, Claire, Judy, Cora, and my brother Charlie came. We were living our family's worst nightmare.

The wake lasted one afternoon and one evening. Because my mother was so loved, many people came to see her and offer their condolences. It was comforting to know and see that she meant so much to so many, but meeting and greeting people was difficult. The funeral, which took place on November 7, was even more challenging. We woke up that morning to an unusually bizarre storm for that time of year. There was snow and freezing rain, and farther north it was snowing much like a nor'easter. Sisters from my community who lived up north started out but were forced to turn back because the storm was raging and the roads were too treacherous. A few of the sisters came the night before and stayed at our community in nearby Kittery. The weather also prevented us from having a ceremony at the gravesite, but the funeral was poignantly beautiful. I will always remember the love, reverence, and the pain of saying good-bye to my mother.

Shortly after the funeral, I drove back to my mother's gravesite to pick up some flowers. As I approached the cemetery, the snow turned to rain, falling gently on the windshield. It had been well over two hours since the funeral, and I presumed my mother would already be buried but, upon entering the cemetery, I realized that I had yet to confront the grave. It would be the second time in a matter of months to bury a family member, and the pain of it seared through me. There was an elderly man who was just beginning to bury my mother's coffin. I couldn't believe my eyes but knew I could not leave. I watched him throw one shovelful of dirt after another into the hole that now held the woman who was the center of my life. I watched as he covered this woman that had gifted me with life. I yearned desperately to be with her. "Oh, God," I whispered to myself, "I can't stand this pain." The pain squeezed my heart like a vise grip that wouldn't let go.

I remember bending down to take some dirt into my right hand and a white rose in the other. Gently I threw them into the grave. I stayed until the old man had finished. I thought, *I'm not going to make it. I have to live the reality of this nightmare now.* Deep in my heart I heard the words "Choose life, Linda. I gifted you with life, and now you need to choose it!" It was my mother's legacy and her blessing to me. My knees were weak, but I managed to walk back to the car. I realized that I now stood alone as a woman. While the arms of many embraced me, the pain of loneliness was omnipresent. A handful of dirt and a white rose thrown into the grave brought home the realization that she was gone and I never had the chance to say good-bye.

My mother was buried on a Thursday, and by the following Monday her apartment was cleared out. We needed to do that, we needed to bring closure, but it was so fast. It was very hard on everyone. Her things needed to be distributed, but I didn't want anything except her rosary. That Monday, I returned the keys to her apartment. I walked into the empty house and stood there. With tears in my eyes, I said good-bye to my mom and my home. I put the keys down, walked out, and closed the door.

In my heart, I was leaving home. Whenever I had come

to South Berwick, I stayed with my mother. My sisters and brother all had their own homes, but this was my home, and now I was closing this chapter of my life. I felt both orphaned and homeless. My siblings were wonderful to me. Claire and Bud extended an open invitation, and each of them gave me a key to their homes. They assured me I would always have a place to stay whenever I came to town. My sister Cora often said, "We're not much, but we're certainly hard to beat." It was true. We have always been there for one another. We're all different, have had our own experiences, and have our own way of dealing and coping with things; but when adversity or disappointment is present, I cannot ask for a more tender, supportive group of people. I feel truly blessed to be a part of them and have them be a part of me.

Linda's Family:
L to R: Cora, Carol, Claire, Judy, Linda, Charlie

A few weeks before my mom passed away, I went home to see her and to spend some time in familiar and loving surroundings. She always treated me like a princess when I visited, and took great joy in preparing my favorite foods and baking all kinds of "goodies." That evening, while we talked, and as she prepared dinner, she stopped, looked at me, and said, "Linda, do you know the one thing I pray for?"

I said, "What's that, Mom?"

She replied, "The one thing I pray for is that I don't die alone." My heart skipped a beat as I realized I couldn't even begin to think of losing her; it was not something I thought I could ever handle.

Shaking off the feeling, I said to her, "Mom, there are six of us, so you will never die alone. Besides, you're going to live to be a hundred. You'll never die alone, because there will always be one of us here with you." I now live with those words and the realization that I made her a promise I was not able to keep. I will never again promise that to anyone. I wondered if she was trying to tell me something, but I had to let go of that thought. She died alone and was undiscovered for more than twenty-four hours. I didn't know if she suffered before she died, but the doctor told us she did not. I hold that thought in my heart, knowing she was not long in pain.

Four days before she died, she called to wish me happy birthday. I was so happy to hear from her. Before ending our call, I wished her a happy birthday for having given me life. I told her I loved her. I thanked God for the opportunity to tell her that much.

The year 1986 was a hellish year. Surgery tore my body apart. Bobby's passing tore open the sadness I'd long kept hidden, and my mother's death tore apart the very fabric of what kept me together—her love. I felt shredded, void of tears, yet riddled with the unyielding pain of grief. I finally saw death as it is: a fact of life. I had understood life and death as two distinct and separate experiences, but were they really so separate? Instead, was it possible that they represented a continuum, a process of growth? The question haunted me, plagued me, and took root inside of me. This was my starting point with "creation spirituality." I felt that the California experience would help to integrate what I had been living the past year. The Provincial Team, however, saw things differently.

Chapter 8

Vision Quest

Through darkness comes light.

The months following my mother's death evolved in a foggy blur of tears and all consuming grief. Aside from the classroom where I functioned well, I cried a great deal and spent a considerable amount of time alone. I could not talk to anyone; I couldn't even pray. I felt overwhelmed with the kind of deep sadness I thought would never end. There was nothing I, nor anyone else, could do to soften its crushing grip on my heart. Even God let me be. With the loss of my mother, I'd come to understand that I'd also lost part of myself. I honestly believed, however, that part of my healing was waiting for me out west in Matthew Fox's Creation Spirituality program.

My mother's absence changed me. It happened naturally and, at first, almost imperceptibly. Slowly, I began giving myself permission to live. It was an emotional adolescence that I had never before experienced. When it came to Fox's institute, it never occurred to me that I wouldn't attend.

The Provincial Team wanted to protect me. The past year had been filled with pain and loss, and my family and community wanted me to look for an educational opportunity closer to home. Now more than ever, the team felt somewhat uneasy with Fox's unconventional program. They believed that there were other programs better suited for me. I knew that I had to make my position clear. I suggested to them that I was discerning enough to know where I was being called and what I wanted for myself, namely to attend the Institute in Culture and Creation Spirituality (ICCS) masters program. I appreciated and understood the team's concern for my bereavement process, but I assured them that I could just as easily mourn in California. I firmly believed that Creation Spirituality would help me deepen and nourish my own spirituality, so I asked that they bless my request. At first, they did not.

I understood the Provincial Team's position, but I also felt very frustrated. Their concern for me was not only for my grieving, but also for my spiritual and vocational well-being. There is always a risk of loss involved in letting a sister, especially a bereaved one, be so far removed from the community. Though the team did not agree with my point of view, they remained open and respectful of my position. In my heart, I felt we would eventually work things out. At the time, my request was causing somewhat of a stir in the community. I think some of the sisters thought my California plan was a little too "creative." *In a year,* I reasoned, *no one is going to care. They'll greet me with open arms and have all kinds of questions about my experience. It simply is not going to matter what they think now.*

The team and I went back and forth, and, after much negotiating and prayerful discernment, we worked out an agreement. The team wanted me to be anchored in solid, theological precepts before going to California. They strongly recommended I take two courses on the sacraments that were being offered that summer at St. Michael's, a well-known Catholic college in Winooski, Vermont. I also agreed to continue the decision-making process regarding becoming administrator of the Christian Life Center and vocation director for the community upon my return from California. Finally, my request was approved. I ended the school year in early June and then attended St. Michael's for the remainder of June and July.

Before leaving for Oakland in August, I was bedridden for nine days. My back had often acted like a barometer for my stress level. Whenever I was on overload, no one knew it, least of all me, and then my back would rebel with excruciating muscle spasms. It forced me to take time off, this time, nine days. My body was stressed, but my spirit was excited and determined to get to California.

A few weeks later, barely mobile enough to travel, I flew to San Francisco and taxied to Holy Name College, home of ICCS. The cab driver, a sweet man, carried my luggage in for me. When I was finally alone in my room, I sat down at my desk and sobbed. I finally pulled myself together, washed my face, walked out into the hall, and introduced myself to everybody.

I immediately felt at home with the program and the people in it. Creation Spirituality brings one through what is called "via negativa, positiva," a journey in which a person cycles through many different places in the heart, producing "creativa." It happened very quickly for me. I faced my mourning by telling stories through art, movement, and words. I walked through the inevitability of death and dying, meanwhile gaining insight into my own mortality. I came to a greater understanding of what I had experienced throughout the past year. As a result, my perceptions changed. I looked at life experiences not as blessings but as events, good and bad, that blessed my life. I will never be able to say that my hysterectomy or my brother's and my mother's deaths were blessings because they hurt too much. We don't go through loss, pain, and emptiness and say they're blessings; however, I could say these events blessed my life, because, as a result of them, I became a different person. I learned to be with other people in pain, to be silent and receptive, understanding that there's often nothing one can say. I learned to lead with my heart.

ICCS attracted many different kinds of people which both surprised and delighted me. I came to know atheists, agnostics, people afflicted with AIDS, gays and lesbians, Buddhists, Protestants, and people from other religions. There were priests who were gay, people who were struggling with religious life, Native Americans, and people involved in the healing arts and alternative medicine. The differences, rather than separating us, brought us closer together in our brokenness, pain, and personal struggles.

One particular class proved both startling and enlightening. It was the African dance class where, like members of an African community, we stood in a circle. Everyone, in turn, was invited to stand in the middle of the circle and share his or her story. I was nervous, but I thought I could manage to tell a little bit about my life. I was startled when we were told to share our likes and dislikes about our bodies! On the rare occasions I even thought about my body, there really wasn't much I liked about it. I suddenly felt as if I were on the edge of a precipice, opening myself up before these men and women, leaping into a bottomless space. I was more than frightened. My nerves felt as though they would jump out of my pores, and I had to remind myself to breathe. I knew I couldn't last long in this agitated state. Getting it over and done with seemed the only solution, so I volunteered to go first. When I stepped into the circle, my heart pounded loudly, and my hands and legs visibly trembled with nervous energy. I knew I was alive, and my body seemed to scream with the desire to share its wounds and vulnerabilities.

This was the first time I had ever described aloud how my skin really felt. I was scared. I began with my face, my eyes, and then my nose. My voice cracked when, for the first time, I admitted how unhappy I was with my teeth. I loved my hands. I loved to touch and to hold, and I believed hands have a way of blessing. As we spoke, we had to touch each part of our body: face, neck, breasts, stomach, and legs. Pain tore at my heart as I spoke about the part of me that had a scar. My womb had been removed; the potential for giving birth taken from me, and I felt an incredible emptiness. As I gave voice to my pain, tears streamed down my face. I stood, hands covering below my stomach where my womb once was, feeling the full impact of brokenness and loss. Suddenly, amidst the pain and the tears came a new feeling of strength, of owning and reclaiming my womanhood. Describing the parts of my body that I loved, parts that I had lost, parts that shamed me, for the first time, brought everything into a new focus. Through my body's story, I was beginning to see who I was and who I was becoming. One by one, the others came forward as I had. We all cried as we revealed our many wounds, but within those wounds, the light of divinity showed through our humanity, our oneness.

My group made the Scriptures come alive for me. Compassion and acceptance for each person's individual integrity was always present, always palpable. We were all different, but in matters of the heart, we were one. We learned to support one another during seminars and practicum. Together we delved into creation spirituality, spiritual psychology, spiritual direction, and deep ecumenism. We also took classes in dreams and liberation, feminist awakening, and the mystics, namely Meister Eckhart, Hildegard of Bingen, Julian of Norwich, and Mechtild of Magdeburg. We shared classes in tai chi, dances for universal peace, arts as healing, creative writing, African dance, and the wisdom of Native American spirituality. Each day was an experience of wonder, expansiveness, and deeper grounding in self.

The most memorable experience of my training occurred during the Native American Spirituality class. The class was taught by a wonderful, spirit-filled gentleman named Buck Ghost Horse. He walked us through a number of Native American traditions, which included a ritual where adolescent boys were asked to make a vision quest. Each boy spent a twenty-four-hour period alone on a mountain, praying and seeking a meaningful quest for his life. To accomplish this, each needed to confront something in himself that, once faced, would allow him to jump from adolescence into manhood. Many of the people in my class were very interested in participating in this kind of experience.

Native American tradition is grounded in nature and life experiences. They use ordinary things and make them meaningful. Nature speaks to the Native American from the trees, rocks, grass, sand, rainbows, eagles, leaves, and even worms. Everything has a purpose, a meaning. I was very attracted to this tradition because it spoke to me of nature, of life, of all of creation and the cosmos. These were things that, as a child, I had loved profoundly. In this class, the essence of spirituality was heightened.

Buck Ghost Horse continued to explain and describe the purpose of the vision quest, announcing that the opportunity to experience it would be offered to students. I immediately thought that it was something I could never do. You could never get me on a mountain, exposed to the elements for twenty-four hours, and besides, I'm scared to death of the dark! A few days later, I had a dream. Buck Ghost Horse came to me and offered the vision quest, saying how important it was for me to make it. I woke up with the importance of the vision quest dominating my thoughts. I even said aloud, "No, not me. I'm not going to make this vision quest," but the dream stayed with me. It would not go away, and it made me think. I wondered why I had the dream. For several days, I wrestled with the dream and its message, and then I thought, *Why not?* Perhaps this experience would bring me to a different place in my journey of healing.

Not everyone was allowed make a vision quest. We

needed to have a purposeful reason for wanting to do it. We needed to express an awareness of our own personal emotional state.

The date was set for April 17, which, coincidentally, would have been my brother Bobby's fiftieth birthday. I arranged to meet with Buck and talked with him about my reasons for wanting to do this. I told him about the dream, about my struggle, and my resolve to make one. "The purpose," I told him, "is to touch the darkness within my own heart and confront it." Buck agreed. Later, there were ten of us who met as a group with Buck Ghost Horse to talk further about what we were doing and where the vision quest would take place. We were asked to find our spot in the hills just outside of Oakland, a spot where we would spend twenty-four hours. With help from a sponsor, I found a spot that offered a spectacular view of Oakland. It was gorgeous. The spot I had chosen was in the open, and my sponsor said, "No, Linda, if it's a hot day, you're going to be in the sun, so maybe you should back up." I moved back a bit so the woods were behind me and the overview of the city was still before me.

I fasted for two days with only liquids: juice, bouillon, coffee, and water. According to tradition, the body has to be purified before making a vision quest. Fasting is thought to be a way of purifying and cleansing the body of toxic energy and material. Cleansing certainly does happen! The first day I thought, *This is going to be bad, because I don't fast very well.* When I don't eat, I usually get a headache. From day one, I talked aloud to myself: "This is what you're going to do, Linda. You're going to be fasting. You're not going to be putting any solid food in your mouth. You're doing this for yourself, and you're doing this to get in touch with what you really need. You're not going to be sick; you're going to be fine." That's how I went into it, and I was fine.

On the third day, I got up early. It was Saturday morning. We met at a sweat lodge. This was a new experience. The heat and steam opened and penetrated each pore, cleansing every cell in my body. While this ritual cleansing was taking place, we prayed. I took what my tradition had given me, and prayed to Jesus and the spirit of my mother.

We left the sweat lodge, and I was taken to the mountain by my sponsor. I brought 150 prayer ties I had made. Each represented someone I would pray for during my vision quest. The ties were filled with tobacco and strung together on a very long string. The string was used to mark the perimeter of my six-by-three-foot prayer space. My sponsor joined me in prayer during the entire twenty-four-hour period, and there was always someone at the base of the hill in prayer with us. People in the dorm, and others who knew we were making this vision quest, would also pray for us and with us. The reverence generated from all these prayers was very powerful.

I first laid down a piece of plastic and then arranged the 150 prayer ties around me in my rectangular space. All of the people symbolized by the prayer ties were with me; therefore I was not alone. I felt safe. We were not allowed to leave our space, but had to remain in the middle of it for twenty-four hours. The only things I had with me were a blanket, my prayer stick, my mother's memorial card with her picture on it, and my brother Bobby's picture. I also had a tiny rock that my sponsor gave to me, which was very symbolic.

Accompanied by my sponsor, my prayer ties in place, I was ready to start. I remembered Buck telling me that it would be very important to remove my shoes as I entered my holy space, my holy ground. I took my sneakers off, handed them to my sponsor, and told her to take them with her. There I was, standing on my holy ground, surrounded by my prayer ties, in my stocking feet. The day was overcast. We had arrived on the mountain at about eleven thirty a.m., which meant I would be there until eleven thirty a.m. the next day. We said good-bye to one another, and I watched my sponsor walk away. We could stay in only two positions, standing or kneeling. I chose to stand, and then I began.

I started to pray. I prayed for everybody, for people I knew and didn't know, for the poor, the sick, for the people at the college, and for members of my family. I prayed for all the sisters, each one by name. I prayed and prayed, and then I reached a point where I could pray no longer. It was still daylight, and I thought, *Now, what am I going to do?* I tried to think only about what was occurring now and became really observant of everything: the sky, the rocks, the ground, various insects, a little ant that was walking up a leaf. I became wondrous of all living and non-living things around my space, and I felt grateful.

It was at this point I thought, *I want a sign. I really want a sign that will let me know my mom and my brother are at peace. Please, God, send me a sign.* I looked up and saw a bird flying around. The bird came toward me, and I got chills all over my body. Another thought came to mind. *If it's really true that both Mom and Bobby are at peace, I want two birds.* Suddenly two birds appeared and flew around me. Being a bit of a skeptic, I had to make sure, so I pushed my request a little further and thought, if this is a real sign; a real sign that Mom and Bobby are at peace, then those birds are going to fly right over my head. I couldn't believe it. The two birds circled back and flew right over my head. I started to cry. I said aloud, "Oh my God, this is my sign that Mom and Bobby are at peace and that they are right here with me!" The birds then flew off toward the horizon. And that was the beginning of something very holy in my sacred place.

The day gradually passed, and I found that after a while the prayer ritual did not seem so important, so I focused on what was meaningful for me. I began using the Hail Mary as a holy mantra. "Hail Mary, full of grace, the Lord is with thee. Blessed art thou among women." I kept praying those words over and over. I noticed it was approaching dusk and the day was coming to an end, so I began to pray more earnestly: "Creator, God, I'm here, and I have to go through this. Please do not send any two-legged or four-legged creatures my way, because I'm not the bravest person, and I will die. Please, God, please don't send anyone. I'm really trying to do the best I can." Dusk was approaching, and I was standing holding my prayer stick when I saw at a distance a four-legged creature. I took my prayer stick and pointed it at the creature. "Please go away," I said, "I am so scared, so please go away." By then, the creature, which turned out to be a coyote, was running toward me, but stopped directly in front of me. He suddenly veered sideways and then disappeared into the woods. My heart beat wildly, and part of me wanted to run, but there was no place to go. It was getting dark, and I didn't know the mountain. I thought, *Jesus, Mom, and Bobby are with you, and they promised no harm would come to you while you're on your vision quest. You need to know that you are secure from here to heaven and nothing will enter your space if you stay in your space.* I put my safety in their hands and did not think about that coyote for the rest of the night.

The weather is usually glorious in California, but not on this particular night. It drizzled, the wind was picking up, and it was one of the coldest nights we had had. The wind was crossing my sacred ground and hitting me in the face. It was cold, and by this time, so was the ground. I was standing in stocking feet on my piece of plastic. My feet, then my legs, then my whole body became cold, and there was no way to get warm, not even with a blanket. The drizzle and overcast completely shielded the moon and the stars. It was as dark as doom, and I was frightened. Then it occurred to me, *I'm here to face my darkness.*

Both within and without, I was in darkness. I was on my knees praying and felt I knew a little of what Jesus might have experienced when he was on the mountain by himself. The fear mounted, and I was feeling nauseated. I began to vomit, but it was dry heaves because there was nothing in my stomach. My head throbbed. I felt myself sinking into my fear, and I didn't know if I would make it out again. I thought, *Here I am on this mountain, I did this to myself, nobody put me here, and they're going to find me dead tomorrow morning because I'm so sick.* I thought again of Jesus when he was tempted, and I understood something about that experience. There was such a great desire to give up. I had never been tempted like that before. The fear that I would not make it through the night was excruciating.

I put my head down, wrapped myself in a ball, and

closed my eyes. It was so cold. My prayers seemed weak, and a kind of surrender moved through me. Then it happened. I felt his presence next to me, and I was flooded with an indescribable sensation; I knew it was Jesus. He put his arm around me as if to protect and comfort me. Something in me let go, melted away. I sat up. My headache was gone. I no longer felt frightened or scared of the dark. There are no words to describe this experience except that it was profoundly spiritual, revealing the power of Jesus and God in my life.

I prayed. I prayed with my heart, a wordless prayer of gratitude. I continued praying, and when I looked up I saw a line in the sky. I said, "Thank you, God, the night is over. Thank you, God, the day is beginning." Everything was lifting, and then suddenly the curtain was drawn, and it was dark again. I had no idea what time it was, and my mind struggled with the thought that it was only midnight ... probably just a cloud. I began to pray again, and suddenly it was morning. I will never forget that moment. I had been through an experience that had taken me into the darkest place in my heart. I had the profound understanding that if I stayed through the night, if I stayed with the experience of pain, something would happen. It's important to stay and not run. I needed to go through the darkness in order to see the light. Daylight came, and it was beautiful.

I realized that this was the gift of my vision quest. I went through the dark, through that desperate place that seemed to have no exit, not seeing where it was taking me. It was a place through which I had to pass, making use of all my strength. I learned that no matter how long the night is, no matter how dark or how fearful it might be, the light of day would come. Day came, and it brought me home to myself. That was my gift. I survived the darkness.

I watched the sun come up, and it was exquisite. Surprisingly, I watched myself in the snare of another temptation when I thought, *God, I can quit now. I've been through the night; alleluia; praise God; it's over!* My goal was to continue praying until my sponsor came for me. I learned that that can be as hard to endure as any part of the vision quest, because part of you justifies that you have completed the hard times, and now it is time to move on. Wrong! It was time to simply continue doing what I had been doing, which was praying. I prayed as deeply as I could, and wonderful things began to happen. I communed with some members of the winged insect family. There were hornets, bumblebees, and flies swarming about saying "Hello!" to the morning. There was a beautiful orange butterfly that flew all around me and wouldn't leave me for the longest time. Its presence was almost angelic, and I felt blessings emanating from its wings right into my holy space. I was grateful and so happy. I felt wiser and closer to who I really was. I continued observing, watching, and feeling gratitude that I had lived through it and learned so much.

My sponsor finally came for me. We were all to meet at another sweat lodge off the mountain. As we left the area, it was suggested that we not say a word, which was a little beyond me. I could not stop talking. At the entrance of the sweat lodge, I remembered that I had had no food for three days. I entered the lodge, and it was extremely hot, the rocks were crackling and the steam rose in thick blankets. It was a different experience this time. I loved it, found it refreshing, cleansing, and was not at all light-headed when I emerged into the sunlight. I went back to my room and showered. We were cautioned to be careful what we ate because our stomachs did not have anything in them. I devoured a hamburger and fries and felt wonderful; however, later, back in my room, I was completely drained. I wrote in my journal for a little bit but went to bed early. I woke up early the next morning and continued to write. I didn't share the experience with anyone for a week, allowing it to sit within me and unfold. At the end of the week, I met with Buck Ghost Horse and talked at length about what had happened.

A vision quest is truly an unparalleled experience. I am not at all sure that it is one I would recommend to everyone because it is very difficult, but for someone absolutely committed, it will never be forgotten.

I remember how upset my family was with me for undertaking the vision quest. They were concerned and scared for my well-being because, at the time, there had been several assaults and homicides in the hills surrounding Oakland. They had said to me, "Linda, go in your room, close the door, stay there for twenty-four hours and pray. It will have the same effect." I knew my sisters loved me, but I had to go through this. I said to them, "I'm doing this because I need to get in touch with part of myself and part of nature," and I did. I got in touch with the elements, I got in touch with my own heart and soul, and I got in touch with my vulnerability and the gift of life. Above all, the presence of God touched me, and I am forever changed because of it.

My nine months in Oakland allowed me to live creation spirituality. I'd confronted my own darkness and fear along with death, loss, and grief. I learned that grieving takes time. It is the process of healing. No one can say to another when it should be over. I am still, to this day, grieving and healing. I have lived it, and it is mine. There are moments when memories surface and the sadness is there. Although it is different, I sometimes mourn my mother more now than the day she died. I miss her face, her smile, and her touch as much as I did then, but time heals. Time allows others to step into your life, to hold you and to be held by you, and to allow you to do what you need to do in your journey through loss. Later, I was drawn to work with people who were dying. I would never have been open to that experience had I not evolved and healed through time and the vision quest. I realized I had changed, yet I didn't know exactly how or to what degree. As I flew back home, back to Winslow, back to the Christian Life Center, I knew something powerful had happened to me. I did not know how it would manifest itself, but in time I was certain it would, and indeed it did.

Chapter 9

Struggle

**Bumps and potholes are life's way
of getting our attention.**

It was not easy to return to Winslow after the Oakland experience. Much had changed within me, and I felt I was no longer the same person. I didn't know or understand the impact of these changes because they had not yet fully evolved, but I knew they were there. There was little time for transition, however, and I was immediately plunged into my responsibilities as administrator of the Christian Life Center and vocation director for the community. These dual roles were a brand-new experience and demanded all of my attention. As administrator of the center, I coordinated the numerous groups that were coming and going and helped to oversee maintenance of the building and grounds. Once again, the need to be focused was important because I realized I was not an administrator type, but I was given a job to do, and I was determined to give my all to that end.

As vocation director, I met and worked with women who were interested in religious life. I shared with them the values of the community, our constitution, and the unique charisma expressed by the Sisters of St. Joseph. The vocation director offered support until the women expressed a desire to enter religious life. The director would then make a recommendation to the formation director. I attended workshops specifically designed for this kind of work and expanded our focus with new brochures and printed material highlighting the mission of the Sisters of St. Joseph. I educated the sisters in the community about our vocational program and gave presentations and talks to groups of interested women. Vocation retreats and weekends at the Center created a reverent atmosphere for exploring religious life and the call one felt toward it. I enjoyed this work, but as with other congregations, the community was experiencing diminished interest. It was a trend that saddened many of us. No matter how many workshops we took or how creative our brochures and retreats were, we couldn't seem to generate much enthusiasm. As I busied myself with a new retreat program or a new idea for a pamphlet, I ignored the encroaching reality we all had difficulty seeing.

During the first year, the center was an extremely busy place, but a decline in the number of groups slowly became apparent in the second year. The popularity of marriage encounters dwindled, and an increased number of parishes organized their own encounters for engaged couples. Various support groups, including cancer groups, were launched by other organizations, and the areas to which the center had almost exclusively ministered were now being addressed by others. Our numbers began to fall. We were feeling the pinch as more groups who rented space from us were unable to afford the weekend costs at the center. We were hard-pressed by the changing times, the increasing availability of services like ours, and the fragile economy.

I functioned well as administrator and as vocation director, but part of me felt a return of the lifelessness I'd experienced when I first worked at the center. I yearned to be more engaged with people rather than with overseeing programs that facilitated and supported others. I was committed to these jobs for a period of time, and I wanted to honor that, but I also needed something else.

Through a program affiliated with the local visiting nurse association, I became a volunteer hospice worker in my "spare time." Hospice volunteers were part of an interdisciplinary team that included a doctor, nurse, social worker, and home health aide. The volunteer provided respite care for the primary care person, emotional support and companionship to the patient and family, and helped with meal preparation and simple tasks or errands. For a few hours a week, the program allowed me to become involved in the most precious and vulnerable time in a person's life.

I completed the nine-week certification course and then worked with several patients over the next year. The program required a minimum of four hours a week, and we were assigned one patient at a time, following that person until he or she died. After becoming involved with hospice, some patients lived for only one or two weeks. I developed a very close relationship with a woman who lived for several months and for whom I prepared light lunches. Following chemotherapy treatments, debilitating nausea was always a problem for her. I ran errands, did things around the house, and sometimes we just talked or sat quietly together.

My patient-friend talked openly and fearlessly about her illness. She knew what she wanted and chose to live as meaningfully as she could. Her attitude was beautiful, and it made me seriously look at my own life and how I wanted to live it. I followed her to her death, and the experience was deeply moving. It helped to clarify the subtle shifts in focus that were developing within me. The spiritual nature of our relationship in the last months of her life filled me with a desire to become a chaplain, specifically a chaplain to the dying. When I look back at my journey and how terrified I was of death and people who were dying, I find God's grace simply amazing. The hospice experience showed me that I no longer needed to fear death; rather, I wanted to work more closely with those who were moving toward it.

I had been at the Christian Life Center for nearly three years and knew it was time to move on, to take a risk, despite my fear of failure. There were no chaplaincy programs in Maine that fit my needs, so I looked beyond the area. I was ready to branch out of the diocese, or out of the state, to get a different exposure. My Provincial gave her support, and in March, 1991, I applied to Interfaith Health Care Ministries in Providence, Rhode Island. I was interviewed and accepted into its nine-month intern program which ran from September '91 to May of '92.

The Sisters of Mercy had a very large convent and residential home just outside of Providence, within easy travel distance to Health Care Ministries. The building was enormous and could easily house over one hundred people. The sisters often accepted "Interfaith" students as boarders, and fortunately I became one of them. I had a room, ate meals, and attended Mass there, but I was basically on my own and came and went as I wished. I liked the arrangement because, in addition to being a full-time student, I often traveled to Winslow for weekend community meetings, and once a month, met with four other sisters with whom I'd formed a community.

The group was made up of three very serious "thinkers," one "feeler" (me), and one sister who was a combination of both traits. We were friends, committed to religious life, and yearned to create something new that would make a difference. We met regularly, once a month, to share our life from various ministries and to grapple with the question of where religious life was heading. We wanted to form something that would energize and incorporate God as the central theme to our purpose. We fortified and nourished each other's spirituality through acceptance, love, and prayer. We were asked, "What are you going to call yourselves?" We decided on the name Chaos Community because of the chaos within our larger community. Chaos provided a space in which to question old familiar securities, the meaning of life, and the authentic sources of human identity. Periodically, it came right down to examining our own uncomfortable feelings and the conflicts we had with each other or within our respective ministries. When sisters first heard about our name choice of Chaos Community, a little furrow would form between their brows, or their lips would tighten and the corners of their mouths would go down and they'd ask, "What are they up to?" They felt something mysterious was brewing because there were a number of strong people in the group. The truth is that we were trying to find our way, just like everyone else. Many sisters carried a vision, a few could articulate and speak for the community at large, but we were all confused as to how to make the vision real in concrete terms. This was our challenge and our mission. Meeting with this handful of sisters once a month was a cherished comfort and support for me as I moved through the rigors of my pastoral internship.

The Interfaith Program was an extremely busy and intense experience. There were classes and seminars in Clinical Pastoral Education that included health care issues, pastoral care training, and an in-depth exploration and processing of anger, stress, and other emotional issues. Three days a week we visited patients at a nearby hospital, and on Tuesdays and Thursdays, we met for classes, supervision, and group discussions. During supervision, we reviewed our interaction with patients through written reports called "verbatims." The verbatim included the patient's age, gender, marital status, religious preference, date of admission, and the admitting diagnosis. We indicated the date, time, and length of the visit, a detailed plan or goals for the visit, and observations made at the time. The actual verbatim traced the dialogue between the patient and intern from beginning to end. Part of our presentation included a personal evaluation and the pastoral opportunity our visit offered. We stated the facts as they occurred, our interpretation of what happened, and our reaction to the experience.

The supervisors were very hard on us and, at times, quite unnerving. We learned a great deal about ourselves, our strengths and weaknesses, and how we could best integrate suggestions for improving our interaction with patients. Other chaplains and peers listened and challenged our approach to the patient. The confrontations were tough, and part of me dreaded them. I knew it was helpful and necessary to develop pastoral skills, but that didn't make it any easier. Rejection and criticism were major issues for me, and they reared their heads during this training.

Tuesdays and Thursdays always ended with a group discussion. There were seven in our group. We sat in a circle, and it was up to us to further the meeting with our discussion. Supervisors were there to observe, but not to participate. The first few minutes were the worst. I do not do well with silence, a lifelong trait that was soon recognized by the group. We had a frustrating little routine going. My peers knowingly smiled at each other, and then one or the other would say, "Just sit here a few minutes, and Linda will get us going." Sure enough, I'd start to feel uncomfortable, and then I'd begin talking. I nearly always started the group. There were times when I was quiet because someone else needed to take the lead, but it was always grueling to sit with the silence in group settings. It didn't take me long to feel at home in the silence of a patient's space, but that wasn't the case in the beginning.

My first day at the hospital was memorable. My assignment was to visit patients, but I wasn't sure what I was supposed to do or say. I walked into my first patient's room, introduced myself, and offered to spend a little time with him to see how he was doing. He totally ignored me. The second patient told me in no uncertain terms that he could care less that I was there. I said, "Okay" and left quickly. My third patient was an older lady who was sitting in a chair when I walked in. As I approached her, I began talking and again, no response. The woman's roommate said, "She's deaf." She hadn't heard me, so I felt relieved. It meant I wasn't a total failure, but that day, nothing worked out the way I had imagined it would.

My expectations of patients and myself were unrealistic. I wanted to enter patients' rooms and have them welcome me and like me. If they didn't, I thought surely I was doing something wrong and blamed myself for not doing it right the first time. During group discussion with my peers, I was forced to look at and address my issues of abandonment and rejection. My difficulties arose with certain patients, with critiques from my supervisors, and confrontations with peers. My reaction to an unresponsive patient prompted supervisors to ask, "Is it important that everyone likes you? Remember, you're walking into someone else's space and these people are not well. It's not about you; it's about them and where they are." More than once I needed to reflect on a patient's feedback, and I slowly learned that criticisms were not personal. For a while, though, it was rough.

Incorrect assumptions were another recurring theme. I remember walking into a room, where the patient was sitting in her chair, and there was a suitcase on her bed. I sat down, told her who I was, and in the midst of the conversation I said, "And you're going home today." She said she was. I added, "You must be so happy." She said, "No, I'm not." She wasn't happy because she was going home alone and was afraid to be by herself. This admission opened up an opportunity for her to talk about her feelings and to receive some emotional support, which she very much needed. It was a beginning. Maybe I could do this, after all.

On another occasion, I was with a woman who had just learned her cancer was inoperable. She was extremely sad and distressed that her little five-year-old daughter would grow up without her mother. The thought that she would not be there for her was unbearable. The situation was heartbreaking, and I was deeply shaken by this woman's story. I had just left her room when I was asked to visit the person in the next room, who was also very ill. I gave myself a minute to catch my breath and entered the room. The patient was in bed sleeping, and three adult sons were present. While speaking with the sons, I said, "This must be really hard to watch your dad's sickness." They said, "Yes, it's very difficult to watch our mother." I was stunned! The woman had very short hair pushed back and masculine features. I made myself go over to her and prayed to hide my embarrassment; nevertheless, the sons appreciated my prayers. The next day, on a return visit, I was a little more relaxed. The sons were happy to see me and never commented on my blunder. As an intern, I was again reminded that it is important to know exactly who was in the room before entering. We couldn't assume that it would necessarily occur to whoever sent us to the patient to tell us everything we needed to know.

Early in my training, when I met a patient who was not interested in talking with me, I wanted to run out of the room. Later, I learned to be more comfortable with myself, and I was able to say, "I understand. It's okay. I just wanted to say hello and see how you are. If there's anything I can do, I want you to know I'm here." Other times I would say, "It really sounds like you've been hurt, and if at any time you want to talk about that, please feel free." Sometimes the patients picked up on the invitation and talked about what they were going through. They'd say, "I've been really hurt by the Church, and I don't want to have anything to do with it." I'd respond by saying, "It sounds like you've been carrying this hurt for quite a while." I spent time listening to them talk about the pain they had been holding, or the divorce they had been through, or how church members had said something that affected them for most of their lives. Many were dying and felt God would not forgive them. I would ask them to forgive themselves and to trust that God had already forgiven them. Some let me know how much my acceptance of their thoughts and feelings meant to them. The imminence of death is always profoundly intimate and real. For those who can talk about their experience, the ego and personality seem to easily fall by the wayside. I cherished these soulful moments with patients.

Sometimes, what I encountered in patients' attitudes was a startling reflection of behavioral patterns in my own life. The need to stay strong and be in control, at all costs, was a habit with which I was all too familiar. Mrs. "S" taught me how to let go of that—a little.

When I first visited Mrs. Saunders in her room, she was lying in bed with her head elevated, watching TV. She was a large woman of sixty-four with short brown hair and beautiful silver-gray highlights. Her soft brown eyes looked rather pensive and forlorn, but she greeted me warmly and immediately engaged in conversation. After I introduced myself, she turned off the TV and invited me to sit down next to her.

Her face was round and swollen, and a large scar from a surgical procedure covered the left side of her face. Her jaw had been reconstructed due to cancer, and her mouth was still sensitive from the surgery, so speaking was difficult. But it was clear she needed to talk. I asked how things were going for her.

"I came back into the hospital on Sunday," she told me,

"because I have an infection in my mouth. I'll be here until they can get rid of it. I really didn't want to return to the hospital quite this soon!"

"Oh? What happened?" I asked.

"I was in here a little over a month and a half ago. I had cancer in my jaw. They had to reconstruct my whole jaw." By now, talking was difficult, and she had to speak slowly through clenched teeth. "I've been through so much in the last few months," she continued, "but the doctor told me they were able to remove all of the cancer cells."

She raised her hand and touched her jaw saying, "Doesn't look too pretty, does it? But you know, Linda, in time this scar will mend and heal. I am just so grateful to God for more time, more time to live, but it hasn't been easy." At this point her eyes begin to fill. My heart was aching for her, and I reached over and touched her hands. I said, "Mrs. Saunders, sounds like you've been through some really difficult moments."

She immediately responded, "Oh, I have! I keep telling myself I have to keep fighting. I promised myself I wasn't going to give up, no matter what! I knew God would give me the strength I would need. I keep telling myself I have to be strong."

When I inquired about her need to be strong, she explained, "My husband died just about a year ago, and I knew I had to be strong. If not, I might just give up, and I didn't want to give up!" Mrs. Saunders began to cry. I reached over, took her hand, and tried to reassure her. "It's okay," I said, just sitting there stroking her hand while she cried.

I said very little after that because words suddenly became unimportant. Just being with her, touching her, and letting her cry was enough. Mrs. Saunders did not have to hold her pain by herself, and she did not have to be strong or in control. She could allow herself to feel all that had been trapped inside of her for months. I felt I was touching more than her hand; I was touching the holy space in which she found herself at that moment. Allowing another simply to be, allowing another to speak and not interfere with the release of tears and pain was to me an encounter with something very holy. I felt touched by grace to be with Mrs. Saunders in her experience.

After a few moments, she looked at me with tears in her eyes and said, "Thank you, Linda." I sensed she was tired, and when I asked, she just nodded. We said our good-byes, and I told her I would see her the next day. She smiled slightly as I left the room.

That day I learned that when we allow ourselves to be held in moments of weakness and pain, we can then allow ourselves to move through that weakness into a place of real strength that reveals who we really are beneath that insatiable need for control. That day, Mrs. Saunders allowed me to really see her, and I loved what I saw.

Throughout the intern program, I had excellent teachers and supervisors, people who were grounded in their own personal experience and faith and who knew firsthand what they were teaching. But the real facilitators of my spiritual growth as chaplain were the patients themselves. More often than not, their experiences and the way they lived propelled me to my knees. So many brought a clarified view of life, facing the reality of their illnesses and expressing how difficult it was when loved ones remained in denial. The first visit with Mrs. Lovely was a perfect example.

Mrs. Lovely was lying in her bed with her head slightly raised when I walked in. She was wearing a hospital gown and a blue and white satin bathrobe. She had blue eyes and a very soft, gentle look about her. Her blue turban highlighted her eyes and attractively covered her hair loss due to chemotherapy. Her room had many signs of love and affection. Cards and flowers filled her side table and a large get-well helium balloon gently danced on the ceiling above her bed.

Mrs. Lovely greeted me warmly when I entered, and we were soon conversing about her condition. I asked how she was doing, and with a touch of sadness, she replied, "Not too good. I'm rather discouraged today. The treatment they gave me didn't work. I have cancer, ovarian cancer, and now there's nothing further they can do for me." I was listening closely. She continued, "I've had cancer now for two years, two really hard years in my life! Two years ago, I wasn't feeling good, and I went to the doctors. I had all kinds of tests and they found *nothing!*" Her emphasis on nothing was strong and carried feelings of anger and helplessness that went right through me.

"Time and time again," she said, "I went to the doctors and still they found absolutely nothing wrong with me. I couldn't stand it any longer. Finally, one doctor advised exploratory surgery. I went through the surgery, and only then was I told I had ovarian cancer."

"Ovarian cancer, Mrs. Lovely, must have been really hard news to hear!" Tears welled up in her eyes.

"My family just cannot deal with the fact that I have cancer," she said, and after a slight pause added softly, "and neither can I. When you're young, you think you're going to live forever. At sixty-two, I still consider myself young. I have a wonderful family and beautiful grandchildren, and I want to see them grow up. This is just not fair."

Her voice trailed off a little, and I asked, "It's not fair?"

She looked at me and continued. "I keep telling myself that I have to keep fighting. I'm not going to give up! I know God will give me the strength I need to keep going."

Of this she seemed certain, so I asked, "Do you believe it is God's strength that is keeping you going?"

"Yes, oh yes!" she said. "Cancer is so hard to deal with. My faith and my belief in God have kept me hoping. I've always believed that God sends no more than a person can handle. Though right now"—her face clouded over as she finished her thought—"I've had enough."

This was obviously a difficult admission on her part. I said, "This is a real tender time for you, Mrs. Lovely. I hear your pain. You've had enough."

She began to cry and whispered, "I have had enough. Thank you for hearing my words and for not making them holy."

"Holy?" I said.

"I use the word *holy* because so many of my friends want me to feel better, so they don't really listen to me. I don't need to hear pious platitudes. I just need someone who will listen and be with me."

When she talked about pious platitudes used by others to deny her pain, my heart cried.

"It's okay, Mrs. Lovely," I said. "It sounds like you have a flood of feelings to share."

"Yes, yes I have," she said, "I'm really trying to be strong for my family, so I'm not talking about my own fear."

Just then a nurse came in to take Mrs. Lovely's blood pressure. She turned to me and thanked me for stopping by and asked if I would come again. I assured her I would. Meeting Mrs. Lovely made me wonder how we feel the need to speak what we think are comforting words to people who are suffering when, in fact, what is really needed is quiet understanding and validation of their ambivalent and often conflicting feelings. I was especially moved by her inability to share her pain and fear with family and friends, feeling that their burden of emotions was already more than they should have to bear. As I left her room, I knew something had happened to me. I wanted to listen and be with her but not to take away her pain or minimize her story. Sickness is not pretty. To witness others facing impending death, to see them grapple with fear and unresolved issues is not easy. If we can enter into their journey, we enter into the sacred mystery of life and death and see how unconditional love ties the two together. Mrs. Lovely blessed my life because she allowed me to live her mystery with her.

Overall, it was not an easy year for people in my group. It was agonizing to explore with supervisors and peers our intimate feelings and emotions—how we choose or don't choose, what we avoid or deny. An issue that was particularly difficult for me to confront was anger. I didn't think I had any. I did realize that, for fear of being abandoned, I never risked being angry. A cheerful, lighthearted person is not supposed to get angry. It doesn't fit the image of a nun or of the giving person I thought I was. Through group discussion, I began to see how much anger and how many "shoulds" and "should nots" I carried within me. Working with the very ill and the dying inevitably moved everyone toward greater self-awareness and undisguised honesty. Memories returned: the deaths and losses within my family, the fifteen-year-old patient in the nursing home of long ago, my own mortality.

My peers confronted my anger openly, and out it came. It showed up when I cried; otherwise I wasn't aware of it. I was even angry with the fact that I wasn't in touch with my own anger! I couldn't believe how it revealed itself in my tears, my body language, and my words. The truth of my anger was totally and completely humiliating to me. I was angry with my father for abandoning us and very angry with my mother for leaving me. People who didn't like me, or I thought might not like me, made me irritable. Patients made me angry when they didn't accept me. I got angry at my peers when they disagreed with or challenged the way I handled a patient, and I really became defensive when supervisors criticized me. My body would tighten up, and they'd immediately inform me of my response, which only served to anger me further. My friend Kevin, a fellow intern, would say, "Get real, Linda." They also told me that my verbatims were "wordy" and superfluous.

I struggled with insecurity my whole life. Whatever I'd write, people would say, "Yeah, so?" or "That's nice. What are you saying?" I worked so hard at explaining myself, but people, and now my peers, would say it's not real. I'd think, *Well, who cares what you think anyway. This is me. I worked as hard as I possibly could to explain myself, and you don't get it.* I was oblivious to the fact that even the most monumental efforts do not guarantee success. Then I'd cry, and I'd realize how angry I really was. Little by little, my supervisors and peers chipped away at that impenetrable protective wall built to shield me from criticism and judgment. I was like a rock being chiseled, searching for the core. Finally, something happened. These exchanges brought me to a profound new reality where I was less perfect and much more human.

I confronted my powerlessness and realized there was nothing I could do to stop death from happening. I was forced to look at how I wanted to live my life because every day is a small death. As I went through this evolution, the topic of my religious vocation came up and subtly began to unnerve me. I had no words, just a feeling that maybe something was not right, but I was clearly in denial. For the moment, the voice was barely audible, small, and unhappy. It would be several more years before I could really listen and tolerate the message of that now very soft voice.

I completed my internship in May and took advanced training from June through the first week of August. My specialized area was oncology and death. The two-month program required an ongoing peer review plus an intensive review before a group of supervisors. The review occurred midway through the program. We were challenged to see if we could really handle death and dying. The supervisory review turned out to be the most devastating, yet revealing experience I had ever experienced. I went in thinking I was in charge; I knew what I was doing and felt I was in control of myself and what I had learned. My meeting was in July right around the time of the anniversary of my brother Bobby's passing.

The meeting moved along. The supervisors asked me questions, and I was confident in my answers. In the course of the discussion, I happened to mention Bobby's death, and one supervisor, George, asked me how I was feeling about that. I said, "I'm okay. I'm feeling fine."

George looked directly at me and said, "You're kidding, right?"

"What do you mean?"

He said, "You've got to be joking; I want to know how you're *feeling!*" When he said that, it was as though he saw right through me and it exposed a tender, open wound. I said I was okay, but he had put his finger right on my denial, and my real feelings surfaced like an eruption from the inner most part of my being.

I began to sob uncontrollably, unable to stop the volcanic eruption of emotion and pain that had laid dormant deep within my soul.

I said, "This is very difficult. I'm sad. It's a very sad time, and it brings back a lot of memories. Death is hard, loss is hard, and I'm feeling empty." I started sobbing again and had by then polished off a box of Kleenex. I looked around, and some of the supervisors were crying. At one point George handed me his handkerchief, and I took it.

Eventually, the end came and there were no more questions. George said, "Linda, you can leave. We're going to discuss you now."

I came out and sat with my friend Barbara, who was there to await their decision with me. She attempted to comfort me while I waited because I was still so distressed and the tears were just below a very thin protective surface. They eventually called me back in and told me I had passed. George said if the interview had not happened the way it did, they would not have allowed me to go forward to my advanced training.

"Life," he said, "is not like that, and you need to be honest with yourself and admit where you are." I cried uncontrollably throughout the entire encounter. Not only had I passed, but something deep within me had somehow opened, and I felt enormous relief. That same day, I also learned I had a job.

Chapter 10

Decisions

> **I lose.**
> **I understand.**
> **I grow.**

In September, I joined the pastoral care team at Saint Anne's Hospital in Fall River, Massachusetts. When I was offered the position, I knew I'd be in the area for a period of time and, with permission from my Provincial, decided to get my own apartment. I had never lived alone before, but there was a growing need for my own space and the privacy to be able to contemplate and focus on what was happening in my life. I needed some solitary time and the flexibility to receive people and to orchestrate an already hectic schedule. With help from my friend Barbara, I found a small apartment in Tiverton, Rhode Island, that overlooked a river and was a reasonable commute to Saint Anne's. By August, I had completed my training and returned to Winslow to settle my affairs before starting my new job as chaplain.

Because it was so out of character for me, the Provincial Team expressed concern about my living alone but blessed my decision and told me I would always have an office at the Christian Life Center. I packed my things and scrambled to find pieces of furniture.

That same weekend, the sisters congregated at our Provincialate to elect seven delegates to attend the community's International General Chapter scheduled in France for January 1993. Customarily, at that time, the general superior and members of her team are elected for a six-year term. In Maine, monthly work meetings had been held all year to discuss the community at large, and to hammer out three themes our Province would present at the International Chapter. The themes chosen were earth, woman, and the impoverished. These themes were then worked into the demographics, employment statistics, and resources of Maine. We also needed to elect a contingent of seven representatives to the General Chapter.

I learned that my name was among several other nominees on the delegate ballot. We voted for one delegate at a time. An invitation to participate required a two-thirds-majority vote. The voting took some time, but it was moving right along until the last delegate position, for which I had been nominated, had to be decided. Then the tension began. Ballots were collected, names read aloud and counted, but it was too close. We had to vote again. Other delegates got in on the first vote, which meant they had the full support of the sisters. Inside, I was dying. Thoughts raced through my mind and collided, creating anger, fear, and shame. *What's happening here? They don't want me to go. I really don't fit in after all.* Without the community's support I wasn't sure I wanted to go. I held my breath. The second round of votes was counted and read aloud. I hated these out-loud votes; they always seemed too personal. This vote was still inconclusive. The vote was too close, and we had to vote again. Inside, distress rippled through me like fingernails on a chalkboard. "God," I prayed, "please let me out of here!" This was an ego nightmare from which there was no awakening. Ironically, it would have been much easier simply not to go to France. I had a profound desire to do all I could to make religious life work for me and for others. I wanted to make a difference, but it wasn't necessary to go to France to do that, was it? I would have preferred eliminating my nomination altogether, but all I could do was sit there and wait until it was over.

Poised at the third countdown, looking out the window, I noticed streaks of yellowish-rose dispersing from the setting sun. The elections should have ended an hour ago. The final tally was in. This time, I received the required majority vote. I think the sisters were tired of voting. Someone turned to me and said, "It was really hard because I wanted both of you to go." Another was less tactful and said, "I felt we needed to have an older person because we already have some younger people going." Perhaps naively, I thought that most people voted on the merits of a person and how well she matched the position. In part, I felt somewhat cut adrift. I left Winslow that evening for the five-hour drive to Tiverton. The car was packed to capacity, but I cleared a little space on the passenger side for a box of Kleenex. I was teary-eyed all the way back to Rhode Island, and I was so grateful to drive up to my little apartment that night.

Until January, I returned once a month with the other

delegates to the Provincialate to finalize our year-long preparation for Chapter. Each time, a new part of me did not feel at home in Winslow, but I soon became so busy and thrilled with my new job that, at first, I hardly noticed.

In 1992, Fall River was a struggling mill city with high unemployment. Many of its one hundred thousand residents had originally emigrated from the Azores, a group of islands off the coast of Portugal. As I got to know my way around, I marveled at the diversity of people and how destiny seemed to have driven me back to the city where my father had been raised. Saint Anne's is a small, acute-care hospital in the middle of the city operated by the Dominican Sisters of the Presentation. Four of us made up the pastoral care team. In addition to our services, we also coordinated different program areas that involved an ever-increasing number of volunteers.

Among the pastoral staff were Sister Carole, the director; Father Michael, chaplain; and Sisters Marie Therese, Lorna, and myself. I was assigned to the oncology unit and clinic on South Three, and periodically was "on call" throughout the hospital. Different kinds of acute care situations made our work very intense. Being part of a team was crucial. We were in partnership with and for the patients, and I loved it. Through pastoral care, we offered patients and their families support in the midst of their pain and suffering. Our commitment was to extend a sensitive awareness and presence to each one. We focused on the needs of the whole person: emotional, personal, and spiritual, including the silent yet powerful language of gestures and unspoken words. We were also available to the nursing staff and doctors because they too were dealing with incredible sadness in their encounters with death.

People of all ages were admitted to the hospital with this terrible disease that took away part of their identity as they had known it. It was as if the roots of their lifestyle, their way of being, were suddenly shattered by cancer or some other terminal illness. Sometimes, at the end of the day, my heart ached from the human drama I had witnessed; however, interacting and working with members of the team and hospital staff was constantly renewing and energizing. We became very close and bonded around the care of our patients and their families. We encouraged and supported one another as we moved with patients along their journey and became genuinely present in their experience. Harry was a powerful influence in this regard.

Harry was dying of lung cancer. He had fought the good fight and had gone through every avenue of treatment available, but nothing had stopped the cancer from progressing mercilessly. He was extremely thin, fragile, and confined to his bed. Harry was alone and having great difficulty breathing. I went in, sat by his bedside, and quietly held his hand. Harry looked at me, and with some effort said, "Linda, I've lived my life, and I want to die." He paused to catch his breath and then added, "Can you help me die?"

I looked at Harry and, holding his hand, and with tears in my eyes I said, "No, Harry, I can't help you to die." He squeezed my hand and whispered, "Linda, just be with me." In one fleeting moment, Harry put it all together with such beautiful simplicity, "just be with me." It's not important what we say or do, only that we be present with our whole being. A few days later, Harry died peacefully, but he had profoundly touched my life with his simple words, which often come back to me.

There were many others at Saint Anne's who tenderly demonstrated life's value through their suffering and their love. Sometimes, as in the case of Teddy, we became good friends.

During the previous two years, Teddy had lived his life attached to a ventilator. Every day, his wife came to sit by him. They were always happy to see each other and were thankful for yet another week, month, or even day together. They loved by holding hands, smiling, just celebrating their time with one another. As a couple, they lived their love, cultivating the beauty and magic that years of commitment and dedication bring. Theirs was an exquisite love story that touched everyone who came to know them.

On South Three, it seemed as if each patient was a unique story of sacred human drama. Both young and old struggled valiantly against the cancer. Some were able to walk out of the oncology unit in remission, while others continued their battle receiving chemotherapy and radiation. When on call, I was available to the whole hospital, including the emergency room, where I witnessed deaths by suicide, crib deaths, massive heart attacks, and a host of victims taken by tragic accidents. At such times, being present to family members, friends, and to the death drama that touched their lives was all that was needed.

The ending of life is always a profound event. Even when we have fair warning, the loss feels tragic and unexpected. At Saint Anne's, I lived on the edge of a new reality, a new understanding that inevitably comes when interacting with death and dying. For me, it took the form of specific doubts and questions. "What is the meaning of life? What purpose do I have in community? How am I fitting in? Do I fit in?" These were not new questions, but since the August elections, they followed me like silent companions whenever I went to Winslow for Chapter meetings. Instead of getting simpler, religious life was becoming more complicated. I do not fault the community for my state of mind. My question was simply, "Where do I go from here?" Within myself, I struggled to make religious life work. In some ways, I wanted to be a savior and to do something to make the community not only survive but flourish. I wanted to make a difference. I believed religious life was intended to "call forth the Spirit" in each one of us and to be faith-affirming in every way.

At the end of January, I found myself walking on the beach off the coast of Locquirec, France. It was a beautiful site for the congregation's two-week International General Chapter. I was by myself, picking up shells and praying aloud, "Oh, God, help me. God, please help me. I feel so empty." My thoughts were so muddled I barely spoke clearly. I went through the motions at meetings and plenary sessions, but I was distracted and overwhelmed with the emotional pain of "separateness" we were experiencing in our Maine delegation.

Since the infamous August elections, the delegates periodically challenged one another with differences of opinion as to how things should be articulated or presented. The conflict occurred when too many of us resisted change or another's point of view, especially while we were in France. Interpersonally, we all seemed to pull in different directions. It was as though we were repelling one another. I prayed for an antidote, but none came. Someone referred to our dynamics as "spiritual growing pains," but personally, I thought we were just expecting too much of each other.

In contrast, our sisters from the provinces of Mexico and India were doing very well. Vocations were up, and missions were expanding and flourishing. Their cohesiveness, camaraderie, and outright love of life were beautiful to see. I wondered if that's what awaited us in Winslow once we outgrew our "growing pains."

Flying back to the States, I thought of the congregation and how much I loved the sisters and our committed lifestyle. Working in my chapter was incredibly difficult and confusing, but I saw it as an opportunity to renew my dedication to make religious life work. I believed the words of our outgoing General Superior in her opening message.

"Along with all Christians," she said, "we are called to be prophets; to be prophetic demands depth transformation, change of heart, change of attitudes, change of lifestyle, change of whatever keeps our focus on ourselves and on our settled ways. It is not easy to accept a move to elsewhere, wherever the Spirit leads. It certainly involves suffering and continual conversion." Little did I know that, in two years time, the Spirit's "elsewhere" would be more than just dramatic; it would be life altering. For now, though, I was very happy to return to work at Saint Anne's. My life in Fall River was far from perfect, but among hospital colleagues, I found a daily supply of encouragement and support, which I sorely needed.

Upon my return from France, I worked briefly with Betty, a fifty-six-year-old woman who had been in and out of the hospital and was failing rapidly due to lung cancer. One evening, while on call at around two o'clock in the morning, I was paged to return to the hospital. Betty's condition had worsened, and her children asked if I would come. When I arrived, her seven adult children surrounded her bed. I walked over and told her I was there and that we were going to say a prayer with and for her. I invited the family to gather and hold hands as I offered a spontaneous prayer. I asked God to watch over Betty during this sacred time in her life and to give her children courage as they watched this moment with their mother. Invoking the prayer taught by Jesus, I invited them to join hands with their mom as we prayed the "Our Father." The atmosphere became reverent, peaceful, and as we neared the end of the "Our Father," Betty opened her eyes very wide, gently closed them, and took her last breath.

The children were distressed and found their mother's "sudden" death difficult. After the initial shock, I invited each of them to remember the good times with their mom and how she had blessed them. This was an opportunity to say good-bye, to bless her, and to ask her for the strength they needed. One by one they came over to Betty, made the sign of the cross, kissed her cheek or brushed her forehead, and asked for her blessings. Each one was visibly moved and felt he or she was both giving to and receiving something very special from her. These were holy moments that the family would always carry with them.

I walked this path so often with patients. We often live our lives as if they will continue indefinitely, and the inevitability of death is far removed from our thinking. The possibility that everything can change in an instant, that life as we know it can end, remains for someone else, but not us; however, when the threat is real, when there are no longer any options left for physical healing, a terrible loneliness descends. Within that loneliness, the failures in one's life, in relationships with others, and with God become intensely magnified. Often, people have very little experience with being loved for who they really are. It's very difficult for us to believe that we are precious in our Maker's eyes. I witnessed this over and over with patients who were approaching death. It is this "dying" need for unconditional love that shaped and molded my understanding of a person's final moments.

I made it my personal mission to do my best to assure that no patient should die feeling he or she had failed in life. It was helpful for them to recognize that we all make mistakes and we all fall but that we're all here to comfort, support, and help one another. I shared the God of my youth, who was so much bigger than the Catholic Church, its laws, and its judgments.

"God loves us as we are," I often said, "and he does not hold grudges. God is forgiving and knows we make mistakes. It is through those mistakes that we grow and become the person we are."

There were times when patients were nearing the end, and though they had not been part of the Church for years, I felt that they still had a desire to receive the Eucharist. In my heart, I knew that I was doing the right thing by being responsive to a dying person's desire for the host. To Catholics, receiving the Eucharist is the focal point of their spiritual life. Jesus would never deny anyone the gift of his body and love, and neither would I. I would simply ask if they wanted to receive.

Sometimes they would answer, "No, I can't."

I'd say, "I'm not asking if you can. I'm asking if you want to."

Some refused, but others would say, "Oh God, yes!" Together we'd ask God to forgive and to hold this moment precious.

I would take the Eucharist in my hand, raise it slightly, and say, "This is the Lamb of God who takes away the sins of the world. Happy are those who are called to this supper," and we would spend a few moments praying together. I offered the Eucharist, saying, "The Body of Christ, my friend." For some, this was a significant moment of peace, comfort, and, in some cases, unexpected reconciliation. They took their last breath with an acceptance of self and of God, which, to me, felt holy and sacred.

Months passed, and my involvement and responsibilities in pastoral care extended and evolved into educational areas. Sister Carole and I coordinated days of recollection in the greater Fall River area for Eucharistic ministers. They were reverent times of prayer, reflection, and spiritual renewal. We worked with deacons who ministered at the hospital, giving them a two-week evening series on the impact of pastoral care. I was so happy and grateful to become involved with the National Cancer Foundation and was invited to give various lectures on the topic of caring and spirituality. I presented a workshop on spirituality to a group of nurses, psychologists, and social workers, and there was no question that interest in matters of spirituality, especially with death and dying, was growing among health care professionals.

In November 1993, I began a patient-support group called Footsteps. We explored the difficult emotions, experiences, and spiritual issues of cancer. The group had a slow beginning, but I continued to meet regularly with whoever would come, even if it were only one person. Word about the group spread, and, little by little, our numbers grew until there were about ten regular members. Because of chemotherapy, radiation, or illness, it was rare that all ten would come the same week. Some had lung cancer, others leukemia, but the vast majority of women had metastasized breast cancer. The group evolved into a safe haven where intense feelings were shared with others who were in the same situation. The women developed camaraderie, a real union and communion with each other. They shared their lives, gave mutual support, love, tears, and their own special brand of humor. Spending precious time with these women was a gift and a privilege.

My sense of compassion was increasingly shaped by patients and their families and their encounter with death. Especially for the families, the emotional aspect of their lives became unleashed, sometimes spilling over into anger, remorse, and fear. Occasionally, they experienced guilt for grieving while the loved one was still alive. Healing on some level was only possible by allowing them to express whatever they were feeling and being present to understand and validate their pain. This was hard. It took me a long time to realize they had to deal with their own anger and that it wasn't my job, nor could I take away their anger. In the beginning I wanted to fix it, to make it right because they asked me to. I thought I had to have all of the answers all of the time. I didn't.

So often, as I entered the room where someone had just lost a loved one, I was bombarded with the overflow of feelings of grief. With a kind of wild sadness in their eyes, they would say to me, "I hate God" or "Why is God doing this to me?" or "How can God, who is supposed to love us, allow this to happen?" I often just listened and let them say what they needed. When they had finished, I said, "I don't understand either, and I don't know why this is happening, but I'm here with you to help in any way I can." Somehow, we would get through the moment without trying to sanctify the experience or make God a God of love when they weren't feeling that way or even considering it.

Ministering was allowing patients to be where they needed to be, at the time they needed to be there, while not trying to change their feelings. When working with people who were grieving, I often used what I had once heard at a conference—the three Hs: hang around, hug, and hush. Hanging around was a sense of presence and being there for the other, hug was the ability to touch when someone needed to be touched, and hush was not being compelled to talk but being totally attentive and connected. When people were grieving, they often needed to be quiet to experience the feelings they had. Presence was the key with people who were hurting, simply touching their hand, holding the silence with them. I observed that people experienced love and compassion more powerfully with silent presence than words could ever convey.

At night when I left the hospital, I thought of my own life, what I wanted to live and what I was actually living. I felt called to live as a sister of St. Joseph, a life that I loved, but in my heart was an unanswered question. I avoided the question because I really didn't want to face it, nor did I know how. Regardless of what I could or couldn't do, I could no longer deny the emptiness I felt deep inside. Each encounter I had with death called me deeper into my own heart, and I longed to be heard and listened to with the same openness and acceptance I so openly offered to my patients. The lifelong pattern of giving to others while ignoring myself and my own needs had evolved into a chronic blind spot that I was as yet unable to see.

As each morning came, I returned to work, continued my life as a sister of St. Joseph, and lived my commitment as fully as possible. I loved and honored my community and cherished the thread of grace that wove my years of dedication and service to its way of life. All that I lived in community helped to mold, fashion, and cultivate God's presence in my being, for which I will always be grateful. The community had been a midwife to my spiritual birth, and then had lovingly and compassionately nurtured my growth into a soulful core from which I could now evolve. Maybe, just maybe, that is why unforeseen events suddenly catapulted me into my hidden self, a place I so desperately wanted to avoid. Maybe, I now had enough inner strength and resilience to tolerate seeing what was really inside of me and what might be calling me to something else.

Chapter 11

Two Paths

> **Choose not to hide beneath that veil of insecurity.**

It had been two months since I'd settled into a new apartment in Fall River. It was a little smaller than the one in Tiverton, but it was closer to work, and it came with a washer and dryer, very prized commodities. Being on my own while still attached to the community was a wonderful experience. I'd learned to stretch in hundreds of practical little ways related to earning a living, running a household, and building on the lifestyle of service I had developed with the Sisters of St. Joseph. Gradually, over the previous ten years, I felt the community needed to move forward and out of the province of Maine. My heart too carried both an inner and outer need for personal expansion. Since the interfaith training in Rhode Island and building on my California experience, I felt the need for that same move forward and outward that I so wanted for the community.

I very much loved my job with pastoral care. I was busy and often worked beyond the end of my shift. It was difficult for me to walk away from a new patient or someone in need just because my workday had officially ended. Sometimes it was the only time I had to call a few patients at home to see how they were doing. Some were recuperating from surgery, while others, such as Debbie, were weathering the ordeal of chemotherapy or radiation treatments. Despite several surgeries and nearly continuous chemotherapy for two years, the cancer had slowly progressed through her body.

I first met Debbie Pestana in February of '93 when she was admitted for hip surgery to replace bone loss due to metastasized breast cancer. It was an early evening visit. I walked into the room. There were no lights on, and Debbie's curtain was drawn. I pulled the curtain aside and found her lying on her back with her eyes closed. I bent over to be in her range of vision and, speaking softly, introduced myself. I didn't know if she was sleeping, but she opened her eyes.

"Debbie," I said, "my name is Sister Linda. I'm a chaplain here, and I just wanted to come by to introduce myself and see how you're doing." She didn't respond but continued looking at me. I talked for just a little while and asked if she would like to receive Communion. She said, "Yes." I whispered a short prayer, gave her Communion, blessed her, then smiled and said "Good night, Debbie." A couple of days later I was on my way to France for the General Chapter and was away for two weeks.

For some reason, Debbie needed be with me, and whenever she came to the hospital, she inquired as to my whereabouts. Because I worked from a roster of South Three in-house patients, I usually knew which patients I'd

Debbie and Lou Pestana

see that day. I didn't realize at the time how important my visits were to Debbie or how much our interaction dramatically changed her attitude. We visited one day for about an hour while she was on the intravenous chemotherapy. As I left her room, Debbie's husband, Louie, caught up with me in the hall and asked, "Do you make house calls?" I didn't know what to say because I had never been asked that before. Louie continued, "You do for my wife what no doctor, no medicine, no psychiatrist could even think of doing. I don't know what it is, but you guys have bonded, and it's mind boggling to me. When you're around, Debbie behaves as if she weren't sick at all. Sister Linda, I will pay you for your time to come to the house if you can."

I said, "That's not necessary. Just give me your phone number and address, and I will call from time to time."

And I did call. Louie would say, "I can't get her out of bed. She doesn't want to get up. The shades are pulled low, and she just wants to lie there."

I'd say, "Let me talk to her." Debbie would get on the phone, and we talked, joked a little, and I'd ask her if she wanted some company. Debbie would say yes, and I was there in an hour.

Later, Louie told me, "As soon as Debbie got off the phone with you, she'd say to me, "Louie, give me my wig, get me an outfit, and get me my shoes. Sister Linda's coming over." She'd get out of bed, fix herself up, and sit on the couch so eager to see you. You two would laugh and visit for a couple of hours, and my wife acted as if she wasn't sick a day in her life. Then you'd leave, and Debbie would go back to bed and not want to get up again. Sister Linda, there are definitely signs of progress when you're with her."

Like some patients with whom I had worked, Debbie never acknowledged or talked about death and dying. The fear and repression were so strong that it prevented others, including Louie; their teenage daughter, Jennifer; and Debbie's parents from addressing the obvious and the inevitable. The intensity of Debbie's denial, over which she had no control, was emotionally painful and paralyzing for everyone. As a chaplain, my job was to simply accept patients as they were and be there for them at the very emotional place in which they find themselves. Acceptance, presence, and compassion are tender medicine for an aching, terrified heart. The painful drama of Debbie's illness eventually brought us together in friendship and in a way I could not ever have foreseen.

In early spring, the Provincial asked me to give serious thought to accepting the position of formation director for the community. Nomination ballots had been sent throughout the community, and my name was one that had been submitted. Another sister and I talked about a new cooperative venture or team approach to formation. The team format would combine the vocation and formation director positions into a shared co-position. Through meetings, prayer groups, and retreats, we would work with women who were considering religious life and accompany them through the decision-making process. Once someone decided to enter the community, we would journey with and mentor that woman in her religious development through to first vows. As a team, we'd work closely with the Provincial Team in developing the shape and substance of the new formation concept.

Current formation was in three stages: first came the Affiliate Program. During this phase, a woman continued to live in her present environment. The vocation director guided the affiliate with recommended readings, retreats, workshops, and visits to local communities. After a period of time and mutual consideration, if the woman expressed interest in joining, she was accepted into the Associate Program. The status of the associate was one of candidacy. She was not yet a member, but by living in a local community she was able to experience the congregation. She continued her professional work, was expected to be self-supporting, and she shared in community functions and responsibilities for the house. The third phase involved a two-year novitiate training in preparation for first vows. This formation period intensified the new member's experience of shared faith with others. Her life was balanced between solitude and prayer and community life and ministry. The novice had the opportunity to study and assess the nature of religious life and the mission and spirituality of the Sisters of St. Joseph.

At the time, the thought was that the other sister, who was returning from a sabbatical year, could easily move to Fall River. She and I could then initiate plans for the team approach to the project. The possibility that the program would be taken out of Maine and into Massachusetts was being addressed by the Provincial Team. Unlike young parochial school recruits of the past, we knew we would attract women of different ages and backgrounds. Our doors would be opened to divorced women; older women with grown children; women in their forties and fifties who wanted a second, more spiritually grounded lifestyle; or maybe even to women who wanted some temporary time with the community. In my view, we needed to look beyond where we'd been and how we previously had done things.

During the previous twenty-four years, whenever the

community had asked something of me, I had immediately been inclined to say yes. If the community had a need and I could fill it, there was no question I would try; it was an automatic reflex. Very quickly, I envisioned this house of prayer and discernment to be one of hospitality and enthusiasm. Our life had to show vitality, something of excitement for people to wonder what we were all about. In the heart of our commitment, we needed to capture the aspect of hope, of mutual support, and zest for religious life, which sometimes was lacking. Without really being aware of it, it was a time of discernment. I was aware of a vague longing for things to be different. We were capable of being different if we just worked at it hard enough and long enough. Some people in community just didn't seem all that happy or excited about religious life. Some shared their evenings watching television programs, such as *Jeopardy* and *Wheel of Fortune,* while others preferred to knit or crochet together. I loved these sisters, but my sense of community seemed increasingly different from theirs. I couldn't see how these activities would carry the necessary energy to attract vocations. I believed we needed something different.

Formation director was an important responsibility, and I was well aware of its inherent challenges. It was a respected and valued position within the community, but it was not exactly a coveted or popular one. Sisters were not waiting with bated breath for this nomination, and several key sisters who had last been in the area of formation had left the community. The discernment of one's own calling, as well as others, often became challenged or clarified through this particular placement. Later, for me, the decision-making process took on a whole new dimension. Unfortunately, at the same time, all of my hidden agendas and unconscious masks spontaneously came undone. It would be six months, however, before I became fully aware of it.

Work at the hospital that spring was incredibly busy. The pastoral team was going every minute. We never lacked for patients, and we had more training groups coming in for workshops and seminars. The chaplaincy was immersed in me and I in it. Over and over, we walked the last mile, the last days, the last moments of people's lives, and with each, we walked this intimate road with their family as well. One didn't have to be a chaplain to breathe in the holiness. It was just there, like a soft holy gift for anyone whose heart was open to it. No matter how often one experiences the death of another, it still shakes the tendrils of one's life. It was always the same, yet it always felt new, like a birth. I felt myself changing inwardly.

During this time, I saw Debbie Pestana only once in a while when she came in for treatments. In between treatments she, Louie, and sometimes Jennifer took vacation trips together. One day Debbie told me, "Louie is always ready to book a trip for us. Wherever I want to go, he makes sure I get there. He says he wants to give me something to look forward to. Sometimes the trips are a little difficult, but we do manage to have fun together." Debbie always brought something back for me. I didn't encourage gifts, nor was I supposed to accept presents as a member of the pastoral staff, but Debbie needed to do this. It was her way of saying thank you. Giving little gifts or souvenirs was part of her language.

Debbie showed her appreciation by giving things, never with words. She could talk about her nails, her clothes, but she never touched the reality of what was happening to her, and that's where I quite naturally tended to go. That's where I felt at home, but you couldn't get there with Debbie. I wanted her to come to peace with her dying, but not everyone wants to respond in that way or even respond at all. I didn't spend a lot of time with her, but when I did, it was challenging. I talked and she listened. She responded to questions, but the conversation had to be pulled out of her. I was glad for both of us that I could speak and that Debbie, more importantly, wanted and needed to hear me. Keeping in touch with her was important because she needed me, but the only way I could bond with her was through prayer and the Eucharist. She was like a young child who was completely overwhelmed with what was happening to her—and no one could stop it.

I had known the Pestanas for about a year when, during the spring of 1994, something happened that drew me closer to Debbie and her family. At the same time, I was involved in serious, sometimes heated, discussions about formation. These two profound experiences ran side by side, never touching one another. Before the end of the year, both dramatic journeys unfolded in natural progression yet never intersected.

I was at the hospital the day Debbie's legs gave way in the parking lot. Louie had driven her to the hospital for her scheduled radiation treatment, but when he helped her out of the van they both realized she couldn't stand up. Louie couldn't hold on without hurting her, so he laid Debbie gently on the ground. A man walking through the parking lot came running over. "Get some help," Louie told him, "go inside and get some help." In less than a minute, hospital staff ran out and placed a board under Debbie. They picked her up, put her on a stretcher, and carried her into the hospital. Debbie had had two hip replacements, but the cancer had spread to the remaining bone in her first hip replacement.

Dr. Shparber, Debbie's oncologist for the past two years, took Louie aside and said, "Louie, I think it's out of control. I'm going to have to do a little more investigating, but it doesn't look very good."

I had been called and met Louie outside of Debbie's room after his talk with Dr. Shparber. His eyes were wide, he was barely breathing, and he was unsteady on his feet. In halting words, Louie told me what the doctor had said and then fell apart. He sobbed uncontrollably and kept repeating, "The cancer's spreading, the cancer's spreading." It broke my heart to see this grown man cry, to see how much he loved his wife, and how helpless he felt to protect her from this awful disease. Then, just as he had done so often before, he pulled himself together and went to call their daughter, Jennifer, and Debbie's parents. His job was to hold the family together. There was something about this event that touched deeper layers of compassion and insight in me. A muted sense of hopelessness permeated the family, compounded by the denial that Debbie's body was in the final process of dying. No one could talk about it, but everyone was living it. As spring moved into summer, Debbie's cancer leveled and became a little more manageable. It was a much-needed calm before the storm.

My monthly interactions with Chaos Community began to intensify over my nomination to the formation team. They knew I could do a good job, but they were also aware that in taking the position I would not be able to invest as much of myself in the group as I had. The configuration of our "community within a community" would change, and so would the aspirations that had emerged over the past couple of years. The whole situation was awkward, acutely sensitive, and seriously heightened conflicts in a revealing way.

The five of us were a closely knit group. There was something very special about each one individually and about all of us collectively. I loved and supported these women, and more than anything, I wanted to work spiritually side by side with them. We had long thought of, and talked about, living something meaningful within our little community. Initially, I wanted to think this way, but I became increasingly less accommodating as I branched out on my own. I felt we were becoming separated from the larger community, which was not at all what I wanted. I felt divided within myself, and nothing seemed clear. I wanted to live a dynamic spiritual life with these five people but not at the expense of the larger community. Taking the formation position was a way of bringing everyone together, somehow creating an easier transition from the old to the new. I knew what I wanted to do, but I had a hard time giving voice to it. It was difficult putting words to my hopes and my feelings.

When I came before the Chaos group, I was trying desperately to come to some conclusions, and I wanted their help to think it through. Secretly, I wanted their full support. I wanted them to give me their unconditional love, but that's not what happened. "You know," I said to them, "I think I'm going to accept this because I feel there's something I can offer. I really feel I can make a difference."

A few kept asking, "What's the difference?"

After the third time, I got flustered, "I don't know what that difference is! I'm not exactly sure how I can make a difference, but that doesn't stop me from trying. I know we need to change, and maybe this is something I can offer." One shook her head.

"Look," she said, "neither you nor anyone else is going to change the system. If you try to change it, you'll get caught in it."

"Not necessarily," I said. They were convinced that change was impossible, and I was convinced otherwise. I certainly wanted to give it a try.

Our dreams and ideas for religious life were well spoken in Chaos, but we never did anything concrete with those ideas. It was not for lack of desire. There was tremendous desire and good intent, but what eluded us was the next step. We weren't clear on how to get where we so desperately wanted to be, so we just kept talking. With formation, I felt I could do something; however, not having their support was painful. Part of me understood their position, but another part, the part closest to my heart, felt once again cut adrift. I was beginning to feel lost and sensed troubling winds were about to carry me to places I had never considered.

Back in Fall River, the other nominee for the new, joint formation position continued to meet with me to negotiate different formation plans. Here too we had differences of opinion, and issues became increasingly more complex. We both preferred to be in a supportive role with formation. Neither one of us really wanted to take the responsibility of director, but someone had to take charge in order to get things moving. With each passing day, I became a little more frantic. I had a vague feeling that something was unraveling, but, true to form, I plunged ahead. I found what I thought was a great rental house for the community, which would meet all of our formation needs. Unfortunately, the owner needed an answer within a week. I got on the phone and tried to present my case to the Provincial. All I could envision was this beautiful, simple house and all the wonderful programs we could do there. All the Provincial could hear was an anxious, forceful, and nervous sister totally focused on getting the community to make this significant decision instantly. In retrospect, I was indeed somewhat heavy-handed, but at the time, I thought I was just being persuasive. After reviewing the information, the Provincial Team wisely decided it was too fast and too soon. In my emotional state though, I saw the team's decision as lack of support for me. The ground beneath my feet was beginning to crack, and all I could do was keep running to my next option, which was to look for a larger apartment for the other sister and myself. My formation partner was temporarily staying in Winslow, and my self-imposed pressure was continuing to build. Then, right about this time, Debbie began to fail.

It was late August, and the Pestanas had taken me out for dinner. Although she didn't eat very much, on the surface Debbie seemed to be doing pretty well; however, I could tell that she was losing ground. It was right after this meeting that she started to show signs that the end was approaching. Hospice was called the following week, and within twenty-four hours all services were in place. I visited Debbie more often, bringing her Communion nearly every other day. We talked that first week when she was still coherent, and, similar to six months before, she gave her second, and last, rare moment of open communication. "Linda," she said, "promise me something. Promise me that you'll take care of my mom and dad, Jennifer, and Louie."

I said, "I'll be here to do whatever I can do, Debbie."

She looked at me, took a breath, and said, "Be there for them." There was something in her words, and in the way she said them, that echoed inside me.

A few days later, Debbie was no longer eating, barely talked, and was slowly slipping away. Two nights before she died, she lay quietly in bed. Jennifer and Louie sat with her, and Debbie's mother was in the living room. Suddenly Debbie screamed out in pain and frantically stretched and reached for her legs. No one knew what was wrong or what she wanted. She mumbled something between screams, but no one understood. There was a lot of commotion in the room, and emotions were running high. She was frustrated with everyone and very much in pain. Louie moved in and began massaging her legs, which calmed her until he stopped, and then the screaming and excruciating pain rose once more. Liquid morphine, prescribed for every two hours, was now given at ten- to fifteen-minute intervals. For days, Debbie could barely move or talk. Now, she was sitting up in bed, reaching for her legs, and mumbling between screams. Louie was beside himself. He finally said, "Deb, what do you want? Tell me what you want."

This time, she stopped, and very clearly said, "I don't want to die."

With tears in his eyes, Louie held Debbie's hand and said, "You know, you've fought the fight, and now it's time to take care of you, Deb. I'm going to take care of Jennifer, I'll take care of your mother and father, and they'll take care of me. Do you hear me? You've got to take care of yourself." She nodded yes, lay back down, and eventually went to sleep. She passed away two days later, on Saturday evening, September 10. Louie later told me that Dee, a close friend who was also an excellent nurse, offered to stay with Debbie during this time. This meant a lot to him. Dee was always present for the whole family, and it was she who confirmed Debbie's death. She said it happened right after Debbie heard that I'd called from Maine to see how she was doing. I drove down that night. Friends and family were still at the Pestana house, but Debbie's body had been taken away. Louie, Jennifer, and Debbie's parents were functioning in a dazed, pained state, as many do during grief. Even when we know death is imminent, the finality delivers a shock of its own.

The following day, I prepared a prayer service for Debbie. The house was once more filled with family and friends. People cried, and I cried with them. The heart is always changed and moved by death in very profound ways. I was working and on call the day of the funeral, and because of my beeper, I sat at the back of the church with another cancer patient who had been very close to Debbie. I left immediately for the hospital after the service. While driving back, I thought of Debbie and her silent, painful struggle with cancer in the twenty months I'd known her. As with other patients, I'd encouraged Debbie to make each moment count. In the midst of dying, I supported her choosing life. I reflected on my own life, and a strange feeling wafted through my body as I drove into the hospital parking lot. I had this strong image of Humpty Dumpty falling, smashing into many pieces, and being unable ever to put himself back together again. The wall I had so carefully built, brick by brick, over the past twenty-five years was about to come down and I with it. It would only take one, small, innocuous shove.

Chapter 12

Choices of the Heart

Listen and you will hear.

We'd been in deliberations about formation for some five or six months, and my fellow nominee's indecisiveness was increasing day by day. I had certain reservations myself, so between the two of us, formation plans moved at a glacial pace. I didn't want to leave my job, nor could I work full time and take primary leadership for the program. It also occurred to me that I was lost without support from the key people in my life, and without that, something in me crumbled. People had been telling me that I was an ideal person for the formation team, but in reality, no one else wanted the job, not even my colleague. For nearly thirty years, the process of renewal had torn up the organizational fabric of religious life, and we still didn't have a viable plan of what to put in its place. Chaos Community provided new and exciting ideas and visions, but they were without a plan to make them real. The larger community offered security and stability, but remained inflexible and unyielding in the face of necessary, life-affirming changes. Again, I felt pulled in two directions and seemed to be imprisoned in a chronic dilemma. My fellow nominee and I were in fragile territory, both of us in need and both evolving, like two peas in a pod. The whole drama forced a deeply buried issue within me to surface, whether I liked it or not, and whether I was ready for it or not.

That September, after the Provincial Team decided against the house, formation was temporarily put on hold. My colleague and I agreed to give ourselves time to live together, form community, and see what would come of it. There would be no pressure, no commitment. My small apartment couldn't accommodate both of us, so we looked for a larger place. We found a decent place in a good location, signed the lease, and gave a non-refundable $100 deposit. The next day, the sister, for various reasons, changed her mind about living there. We were $100 poorer and back to square one! I could have said, "Okay, let's check out something else," but instead, something in me screamed. I was pushed to the edge of my own effort at trying. I thought, *This is awful! I can't do this. I can't do this anymore! The community voted me in, but I'm not getting any support from the people from whom I most need it!*

I somehow felt victimized by what was happening, and I didn't understand why I was unraveling. I felt broken. I had been trying for so long to fit in. I helped whenever and however I could, and now everything was held back. I felt that the support was not there. It all became magnified in my mind. In my room, I thought aloud, "I've had it with everything and everybody. I don't want formation, and what's more, I am not even sure I want religious life." My hand covered my mouth in shame. Oh, my God, I'd said it! I never wanted to say or think this. I'd always fought against the feeling by trying "to fit into" religious life. I never wanted to leave, and here I was thinking of leaving. A parade of questions marched through my mind. What's going to happen to me? Where am I going to go? What am I going to do? How will I support myself? I couldn't answer any of these questions. I only knew I couldn't do it anymore. I was reaching the end, getting closer and closer to making the hardest choice of my life. In my heart I knew I would leave. The "when" and "how" terrified me.

By the end of September, things over which I had no control had been set in motion. At home, I cried and anguished over what to do, but in the morning, I put on my cheerful, bubbly self for work and dispensed encouragement and positive strokes to others throughout the day. I was busy with patients and various meetings, including my biweekly cancer support group and Footsteps. After Debbie's funeral, Louie returned to the group for a while. The women loved it and were so happy to see him. He wanted them to know they weren't forgotten, and that he was there to support them. After everything he'd been through, Louie also needed support, and I suspected he received it by being there. It was about this time that Louie took me to the cemetery so I could see Debbie's grave. He needed to return, and I think he preferred not to be alone. Being there was terribly hard for him, and he began to cry. Instinctively, I walked over and put my arm around him for comfort, but, at that moment, something happened inside of me the moment we touched. I knew I had feelings for him—feelings that a woman can have for a man. Oh, God, where is this coming from? I was more frightened than I had ever been in my life, and I did not want to deal with it. My life was already too confusing and terrifying without adding this! It was too much, just plain too much. Plus, I had already reasoned, when the time came to leave community, I wanted to leave this place and go where I wasn't so well known. I didn't want to see disappointment in people's faces. It was bad enough that I had to face myself feeling as though I had failed.

My formation partner returned to Maine the first weekend of October. Before she left, we talked at length. I told her of my confusion. I said, "Sometimes I don't know if we in community really love one another. We seem to have such a hard time supporting one another or being happy about our successes. I feel so much more alive here in Fall River working at the hospital than I do back in Winslow." She understood what I was saying, and I continued, "I don't know where I am right now. My whole life is being turned around here. I have all these feelings. I feel in crisis about religious life. I also have feelings of being attracted to someone, and I don't know where it's all coming from." This part got her attention.

She asked, "Does the other person know?"

I said, "No, he doesn't know, and it could be that my feelings will pass."

She added, "I think you should get some counseling about all of this." I totally agreed. I knew I needed help. I also knew she was hurting and needed to figure out where she was with all that had happened over the past six months.

I said, "When you go back this weekend, talk to whomever you need to talk to, do what you need to do for yourself. If you need to, let them know about me. If you feel you can't come back here, it's okay."

I don't know what I was thinking, but for some reason I thought she'd come back. I figured she'd be with me and not leave me alone in my struggle; however, neither of us was in a position to help the other, and after much deliberation, she decided to stay in Maine. She came back for her things and left Fall River. This was it, my moment of truth. I was all alone. I didn't feel attached to the community. I didn't fit and didn't think I could live in it anymore.

The thought of leaving religious life terrified me, but I could no longer ignore the fact that these thoughts had plagued me for a very long time. I was Humpty Dumpty, and I felt broken and scattered. The prototype of the perfect religious person I had always envisioned myself to be literally fell off the wall. The Sister Linda, CSJ, image fell, was shattering, and I was powerless to put her back together again.

In my solitude, I cried. I had lost the ideal, the fantasy of the kind of religious person I thought I was, and the pain was unbearable. I somehow pulled myself together to go to work every day, only to come home and fall apart all over again. While off duty and alone, I cried most of the time. I lost weight, and my eyes were puffy. I didn't have the benefit of makeup, so I hid behind a perpetual toothy grin. It was so contrived; it was pathetic. I was dying inside, but in front of others, I smiled as if everything were wonderful. I just couldn't let anyone at work or in the community really see the terrible mess I was in. The lifelong compulsion was to show only what was good and perfect. In the past, I had been able to support the illusion, but it would take some time before I realized it was now useless.

I shared these experiences with my spiritual director, who strongly recommended I seek counseling, and a close friend referred me to a psychologist. I needed to get to the bottom of this and was relieved to get help. I only saw the psychologist three or four times, but that first visit is engraved in my memory. He asked a little bit about where I was coming from and what was going on. I couldn't talk without crying, but I managed to force a few things out.

"I'm in a vocation crisis," I said. "I'm really struggling, and I think I need to leave, but I'm not clear why I can't, or if I should leave religious life. It's been sitting inside of me for a number of years, and, until recently, I've been able to ignore it." I told him about formation and how it brought this truth to the surface. I described how I had always worked hard to be the best sister of St. Joseph, and how that constant and continuous effort masked what was really going on inside. "I don't know what's happening," I said. "I think I need to leave. I'm not happy, and I feel I don't belong anymore. Maybe it's just a hard time now, and maybe I need to sit with it." I felt I had an entire lifetime of squelched feelings suddenly filling up and spilling over.

My first session ended, and another box of Kleenex was gone. The psychologist gave me homework I was not expecting. He put it this way, "Linda, I invite you to go home tonight and to sit quietly. When you feel ready, I want you to go into the basement of your heart and see what's there. I want you to look deeply within yourself and find what needs to be looked at." He warned me, "You're going to face a lot of things, so be prepared as you venture into this unexplored part of your soul. There's no return, Linda. There's no return. You need to go inside."

I left his office shaken by all that had come out of me, and then I thought, *My God, I'm not very good at going inside.* I didn't think anything would come out of my homework assignment, but I was ready to try anything to get at the truth. That night, I sat on my couch and decided I was ready to try. I pulled my feet up around my chest and hugged my legs. I closed my eyes, took several deep breaths, and allowed myself to unlock a door and step inside. I found myself walking down a long deep stairwell filled with cobwebs. When I reached the bottom of the stairs, I saw a huge trunk at the end of the room. I edged my way over to it. There was a dark coverlet over the trunk on top of which lay a thick blanket of cobwebs. There was an amazing clarity to this experience. It felt so real, and even the basement smelled dank and musty.

Anxiety rippled through me as I moved closer. I pulled one corner of the coverlet and let it slowly slide to the floor, exposing an old, dark leather steamer trunk. Two voices in my mind loudly vied for my attention. One kept saying, "You've got to open this trunk. You have to open it."

The other voice was equally intent. "No, don't. Don't do it."

The first continued, "You've got to open it."

The second replied, "No, I can't."

"Yes! Yes, you can. Do it now!" With a trembling hand, I gently lifted the lid and looked inside. It was dark, but tucked in all four corners of the trunk I saw fear, nothing but fear—my own fear. *Oh my God,* I thought. *Is this what has been stopping me all this time?*

I stood before the trunk and realized that, since my earliest years on the farm in South Berwick and throughout my time in religious life, I had put every ounce of fear into that trunk. In each corner, I recognized not only my own fear but a large dose of my mother's fears, which I had assimilated since childhood. I had absorbed her tremendous anxiety and fear of what other people would think and say, and I had made it my own. It was now in my trunk, and it was my fear, all of it. The thought of leaving community was paralyzing, so the thought was never allowed. Unconsciously, I'd created an image of a perfect religious person who always smiled, saw everything as wonderful, and never said no.

The image of Sister Linda looked good, and she genuinely meant well, but when the trunk was opened, it showed how much of her was not real—not authentic. The need for perfection was all that held the fear at bay. Only perfection would guarantee some semblance of acceptance, of "fitting in." It was all there in front of me. I feared what other people would say, feared their rejection, and feared what was going to happen to me. I was terrified that leaving might not be the right decision, yet everything in me anguished at the thought of staying. I was imprisoned by fear and what it had done to me. As soon as I realized I had a choice, a small light radiated from inside the trunk. Choice, it was about clear, authentic choice.

Left unchecked, fear had a power that robbed me not only of the moment but of my entire life. I was afraid of what other people would think of me, of hurting someone, or of making a mistake. Accepting it involved making a clear decision to claim my past as my own and as part of who I am. It meant being true to my real feelings.

As I looked at the contents of my trunk, again I cried. I became immersed in overwhelming grief for a lifetime of fear, fantasy, and false image. I cried for the unconsciousness of the past and the profound awakening of the present. I moved toward acceptance of my true being and the need to make a life change. It had been waiting for me for a very long time. I could no longer live as a sister of St. Joseph, and once that decision was made, I felt a complete and joyful freedom for the first time in my life. However, the sense of liberation was bittersweet, a mixture of joy and pain—pain for what I knew would lay ahead of me.

I met with the psychologist several more times to determine the best way to approach my departure. I continued with spiritual direction, and when I was clear in my own heart, I contacted my Provincial and asked to meet with her in person. She came down in October, and we talked for a very long time. I explained everything as clearly as I could, how taking a position of discernment had pushed me over the edge. Sooner or later, it would have happened. The truth of my image and its "fall from grace" was inevitable. Sharing this was very difficult, very painful, and we both cried. I needed to speak frankly and truthfully, and the Provincial really heard me.

"Linda," she said, "I want to invite you to take a deep breath and plunge into the real work now of shaping your new possibilities. It's important for you to direct your energies toward a new life." Her acceptance and compassion covered and protected me like a blanket of mercy. My fear dissolved in our tears. In the end, she asked me to take more time to reflect and continue going for counseling, which I did, but the decision had come from my heart and seemed final. I'm sure that outwardly it appeared things were happening very fast. However, on the inside, they clearly were not, and we both knew it. A few weeks later, I met with the Provincial again and told her I was definitely leaving. Fear was what was holding me, and I couldn't be bound to it anymore. Now I had to prepare for the secular world.

I chose to leave, and part of me was still terrified to take the leap into the consequences of my decision. Identifying my fear was only the beginning. This terrible fear had very deep roots, and each one needed to be extracted. It was hard. It was hell. It was death to the image that had been created to protect me, and it met its demise kicking and screaming. For me the course was set, the train was moving, and I wouldn't be able to get off until it reached its final destination.

I continued working with oncology patients who were continually confronting life-and-death decisions: whether or not to submit to a new chemotherapy series or additional weeks of radiation, whether to desperately grasp at any last ray of hope or resign themselves and prepare for the inevitable journey that lay before them. I stood with them and talked from a new place within myself, that fragile place of trying to choose the best path toward healing.

In my free time, I spent hours at home crying, grieving my own loss. I wasn't interested in food and was losing more weight. I felt I couldn't share what was happening with anyone at work for fear it would interfere with my ministry and work relationships. I increasingly grappled with the fact that I seemed to be leading two lives: my muddled, fearful, personal journey and my cheerful work persona. I had to notify many people by phone about my decision. It certainly was not how I wanted to do it, but because I was working so many hours, it was not possible to do it in a more personal way. I only wished that they would understand. I called my friends in Chaos Community and arranged to meet with them individually. I couldn't talk about this over the phone with them. The group was not happy and said, "No, don't do it. Linda, don't go."

I said, "I have to do it. This is it. It's not something that happened overnight, though it seems as if it did." My family in South Berwick was totally supportive and offered to help in any way possible. Without hesitation, they showered me with love and acceptance, which made me realize how grateful I am to have them in my life. However, my decision to leave was very disappointing for the sisters in Maine. I know they felt betrayed because a few months before I'd said yes to formation and now I was leaving the community. They had no warning that there was anything wrong or that I was unhappy. Having everyone believe that everything was fine was a huge part of the image I tried so hard to sustain. I cried a river of tears over having unconsciously misled them.

I had decided to leave my job at Saint Anne's and the Fall River area by the end of the year. I planned to stay with my family in Maine and allow myself some time to think through the next move. I waited until December to tell the hospital staff and patients that I was leaving. I simply told them I was moving back to Maine. Except for my coworkers and a few close friends, I was feeling too broken and vulnerable to tell people I was leaving my community. I knew that if people didn't understand I would not be able to cope.

Had I to do it all over again, I may have handled it differently. Right or wrong, I knew of no other way. I did the best I could under the stressful circumstances, but I felt exposed, insecure, and raw. I didn't think I could deal with the slightest insensitivity or misunderstanding. There was some unfortunate fallout, but ironically, not so much for leaving community. Some sisters, coworkers, and others were convinced I left because I had fallen in love, a perception that really sharpened their tongues.

Around mid-November, Louie invited me to dinner with Jennifer and his in-laws. When the time came, everyone, except Louie and I, begged off for various reasons. When he came to pick me up, I invited him into my apartment, which he'd never seen before. I wanted to share with him what had been happening. I'd known Louie for nearly two years, considered him a dear friend, and felt safe sharing this part of my life with him. Surprisingly, it took all I had to tell him of my decision to leave religious life. With the community and my family in far-off Maine, I was feeling increasingly isolated and really needed to talk to someone. It was then that I felt the depth of Louie's kindness and compassion. The man was not only supportive, but he really heard the pain in my voice as I described my journey. I felt that he saw and heard me in a way I'd never before experienced. I was conscious that it had not been very long since Debbie's passing, and prayed I wasn't overburdening him with my problems.

Out of nowhere, Louie asked, "You're not leaving for me, are you?"

The question stunned me, and I said, "Oh, no. No." Later, when he asked again, it occurred to me that maybe he had feelings for me too, which left me numb and speechless. It was as if we were both on a predestined path of new and foreign emotions. Our friendship was at a crossroads, and it was a paradox of sentiments. We went to dinner feeling that something wonderful was happening. We talked a great deal and ate very little, but I felt ashamed. I'd just told this man I was leaving the community, and here I was eating dinner with him. It was overwhelming, and I was a mess. The next morning when he called to see how I was since we had talked so late, my stomach felt awful, but I told him I felt wonderful, and I did.

December was a month for correspondence. The Provincial had written on my behalf and supplied me with all the information I needed for my dispensation. There was no delay. I wrote to the mother house in France and sent them all my papers. I wrote a formal letter to the pope requesting dispensation from my vows. I wrote to all the sisters in Maine, which was especially difficult. There is no painless way to leave any community. I was taking care of all of that, plus ending my position at Saint Anne's, saying good-bye as best I could and trying to work out where I was going after I left the hospital.

Meanwhile, my relationship with Louie continued to grow. Warmth, support, and presence were his constant gifts to me. He was my sounding board for the next step, for what I needed to think about and how to remain focused on all that was positive in my life. He really couldn't offer any advice, but he was there, present, and aware of my journey. There were times when all I did was cry; that's all I could do. Everything about our relationship was secretive, therefore tense. I was still working at the hospital and officially still part of the community. Even though I was leaving and papers were being processed, I didn't want anyone to get the wrong impression of a sister of St. Joseph, or of me. I didn't dare go any place with Louie for fear of causing scandal. Ours was a blissful, happy courtship, but it was all but hidden from everyone.

On February 2nd, the official papal endorsement dispensing me from my vows arrived in Winslow. It was exactly twenty-five years to the day since I had entered community. When I arrived to sign the papers, I thought I would get very emotional, but I didn't. I was clear, and I was ready. Signing those papers was what I needed to do, and I was fine.

I had never known how important it was to listen to one's self. No one can teach another how to listen. It comes from that place in the heart that brings one peace. It's the same place where I ultimately found my God. It was only through God's help that I was able to endure the year ahead of me.

Chapter 13

Integration

Healing comes from within.

Leaving religious life was the hardest decision I ever made. It would have been so much easier, less emotionally shattering and difficult, to spend the rest of my days in community. Total avoidance would have been my choice in the past. The slightest sign of pain or discomfort, the lifelong penchant for denial while wearing a winning smile was the way I chose to live. That strategy wasn't working anymore, and probably never really did. Over the past year, I'd learned that when the soul awakens its painful journey will not be denied, much to the chagrin of the physical body.

I spent the first three weeks of 1995 in a "transition fog" while packing my belongings and terminating my residence in Fall River. There was a lot to do with the apartment, and I knew I needed to communicate with the people in the area with whom I had had a personal as well as a professional relationship. I had pushed my body to the limit, and, in much the same way as had happened in Auburn and then Winslow, I was out of touch with my physical distress signals, and now I was experiencing a physical mutiny. After I'd left Saint Anne's at the end of December, my health slowly began to deteriorate. I was having lower back pain and developed a urinary tract infection that seemed completely and indefinitely resistant to medication. Later, I suffered headaches, sore throats, and a debilitating pain on my side. I'd been under stress the whole year, and my body was in open rebellion.

At the end of January, my sister Cora and her husband, David, came to Fall River and helped me with the move to New Hampshire. They welcomed me into their home and provided a wonderful space for me to rest and think. Their love and support comforted me during those very difficult days, and they, like the rest of my family, were outstanding in their acceptance and were infinitely gentle and understanding with my healing.

The community was also very generous with me in my departure, which touched my heart. From the onset of my departure process, the Provincial was remarkable in her compassion and kindness, and I will always love her for that. Her attitude and focus sculpted a new space for a former religious woman, so that in our personal confrontation and choices, we were no less a part of the lives of the sisters.

I'd always loved the community. Part of me was profoundly affected by its charisma, and that part of my soul will always be a sister of St. Joseph. The Provincial saw it, welcomed it, and blessed me in my new life. She understood this was not a divorce but a necessary change in my soul's journey that neither I, nor anyone else, could alter.

The transition from religious to civilian life was, at first, very difficult. Without the image of Sister Linda, which had meant everything to me for twenty-five years, I felt vulnerable, and I feared the reactions of others. Physically, I was drained, but my spirit felt very alive as I adapted to the surety of my decision. Life was very different now, and I realized that I was being challenged to recreate my life into something brand new.

Louie's presence in my life was a true gift. I cherished this man with his wonderful joie de vivre and very infectious laugh, but it was really his character that I fell in love with. On so many occasions, I had witnessed his devotion to Debbie, his attentiveness to her needs, and his desire to make every moment of her life special and memorable. He treated his wife with honor and respect, which was very different from how I'd seen men behave when I was growing up.

His sensitivity, however, touched me the most. Louie cried and shared with me the anguish and fears surrounding Debbie's illness and death. He was fiercely protective of his family, and it tortured him to realize that he was powerless to shield Debbie, or anyone else he loved, from the devastation of cancer. I felt completely safe with this man.

Our relationship grew out of mutual respect and appreciation for who we were as people. We had seen each other at our best and at our worst, had enormous respect for one another, and we had a solid history based on friendship and support. Though we were now very much in love, we each still had to navigate through some very difficult emotions.

Louie was still grieving Debbie's loss and felt some understandable ambivalence toward his feelings about me. He struggled with guilt when he presumed people would say, "It's too soon." I was also grieving the loss of being a sister for so many years and was trying to come to terms with the dramatic changes in my lifestyle. I was excited and thrilled but very confused with all that I was feeling. Falling in love in God's chosen time remained a real mystery to both of us, but we trusted God and the new path that was gradually being revealed to us. We knew our relationship was a good thing, a very good thing.

The most challenging experience Louie and I had was telling people, especially his family and friends, about our relationship. We didn't want to hurt anyone, so we were particularly sensitive to the feelings of Mary and Sid, Debbie's parents. They had known me as the Sister Linda who had helped and befriended their daughter for the last two years of her life. We knew it would take time, patience, and understanding for them to offer us their blessing and approval as a couple; however, the person we were most concerned about was Louie's daughter, Jennifer.

Like Mary and Sid, Jennifer had known me as Sister Linda and as her mother's friend from Saint Anne's Hospital. Her father spoke to her about us, and some time later, she and I also spoke. As I needed to express my thoughts and feelings directly to her, I went to their house to spend time with her.

"Jennifer," I said, "I don't understand why all of this has happened, but it has. I want you to know that I care a great deal for you and I love your dad very much but I would walk away from this experience if it were going to hurt you or your relationship with him in any way. You are both too important to me. I need you to hear me say that and understand that I mean it."

Jennifer said, "Linda, I was a little surprised when Dad first told me, but I'm okay now. I just needed a little time."

I nodded and then added, "Jen, I'd never try to take your mom's place. The only thing I can do is be Linda for you, and I'll always be here for you. Do you hear me, Jen?" That was our beginning.

My first evening out with Louie's brother, Fred; his wife, Carmen; and their friends was memorable. I was nervous, anxious, and eager to be accepted and loved as part of a couples' world. I was forty-six years old and not at all accustomed to dating or "going out" with a group of men and women. They turned out to be simply wonderful people. Within a short time, I felt accepted and welcomed, and I gratefully noticed how happy they were for Louie and me. It meant a lot to both of us. After that evening, we began to tell others about our developing relationship. Many were happy for us; some were not, but we quickly learned to create a new life surrounded by people we loved and who loved and supported us.

Louie and I met on weekends. I needed the week in New Hampshire to reflect on these new feelings and experiences. I drove to Fall River on Friday afternoons for an appointment with my chiropractor and then spent the weekend with Louie and Jennifer at their home in nearby Swansea. During the week, Louie and I talked on the phone at least once, sometimes twice a day. It got to a point where we wanted to be together so much that I started making excuses to come down earlier on Friday or sometimes Thursday mornings. Motivated by our mutual feelings, I was excited and full of happy anticipation. All of these new emotions felt wonderful!

Surviving an aching back, facing my own fearful projections, and living out of a suitcase were not easy. Every weekend, I battled the feelings of anxiety worrying about what people would think about my staying in Louie's home. In my heart, I was completely comfortable with what I was doing, but the inner critic in my mind was still merciless. Despite our very kosher arrangement with a daughter in the house, I continued to feel pangs of guilt. We had separate bedrooms, honored each other, and above all, Louie respected who I was.

News of my weekend jaunts traveled quickly throughout Saint Anne's, igniting some hurtful rumors. Comments such as "She is a real disgrace to the community" infuriated me. It was particularly painful because I had never done anything to harm the community, nor was I doing anything to dishonor it now. How could I dishonor something that was part of my very soul? Like a broken refrain, I repeatedly said to Louie, "Those who know me will understand, and those who don't will make judgments; there's no amount of talking that can change that."

Because Louie was also getting hurtful reactions from some of his friends, we supported each other through this difficult time. We reminded each other that, overall, people were very supportive and happy for us. There was only a handful of individuals who, for reasons of their own, disapproved of our relationship.

One day, I overheard Louie tell a friend, "I did everything I could for Debbie. I made sure she enjoyed life right up until the end, until there was nothing else I could do. I don't feel I did anything wrong by falling in love with Linda. She's a wonderful person. It wasn't pre-planned, and I've nothing to hide. It just happened. It's not too soon for me to get on with my life, and maybe someday we'll all find out why things worked out the way they did." Like Louie, I too didn't know why he came into my life when he did. I only knew that he was one of God's greatest gifts to me. Having someone there to hold me, who was exceptionally sensitive and caring, and who accepted me unconditionally was a most precious gift.

By April, I knew my back wouldn't handle driving back and forth much longer. I had pain in my upper and lower back, bladder problems, and was physically exhausted most of the time. Commuting was becoming too difficult, and I entertained the idea of getting an apartment near Louie's home or, perhaps staying with friends. When Louie invited me to stay with him and Jennifer, I immediately felt tremendous anxiety. I thought, *My God, here I go again, wondering what people are going to say or what they're going to think.* I knew I had to trust my heart and do what I needed to do. Louie and I both knew our love was real and that we would eventually marry. Late October seemed to be a respectful date for all of us. It was important to Louie, Jennifer, and me that a year's time elapse since Debbie's passing before making a formal commitment to one another. It was also very important for Debbie's parents. Our relationship was moving very fast for them too.

Moving in with Louie and Jennifer required an enormous adjustment for all of us. The house was very much a family home. Everything there linked Louie, Jennifer, and

Debbie. I needed to give myself time to adjust and also time for them to adjust to my being there. Debbie loved cats, and they were everywhere in the decor. There were cats all over the place: cat frames, cat pictures, cat trays, cat wall hangings, and more. At first I was afraid to do anything, but I needed to feel that I fit into my new surroundings.

In her quiet way, Jennifer was very accepting. I'm sure it wasn't easy for her. Her mother had been ill for nearly five years, had passed away less than a year ago, and the changes of the past few months were being thrust upon her. I tried to be very sensitive to her feelings. In all honesty, some days it wasn't easy, and I felt quite uncomfortable. Jennifer was not very talkative, and I wasn't sure how she felt or what she thought of the situation. On the surface, she seemed happy with my presence, so gradually I unpacked my things and began to let it become home to me.

Louie was terrific. He said, "Linda, this is going to be your home. You need to feel you're a part of it." He gave me total and free reign. The first thing I did was reorganize the cupboards in the kitchen and bathroom, but only after we were married did I make more visible changes throughout the house. The cats, I'm pleased to say, have been retired to storage for Jennifer, should she want them someday.

The pain in my back softened a bit once my commuting days were over; however, it never quite left me, and by late May, the pain returned with a vengeance. One morning, I woke up to find that I couldn't bend to make my bed. I had to kneel, keep my back straight as a board, and make my way around the bed in that position. Louie was worried. I didn't want my back to be a problem for anyone and decided to just cope with the pain as best I could. My resolve weakened as the pain worsened.

By the end of June, I went to a doctor who thought I had arthritis, prescribed medication, and recommended I go for physical therapy. It sounded like a good plan, but two days later, the pain worsened. Louie insisted I get a second opinion and have X-rays taken. While waiting to be seen, I stood in the waiting room with tears in my eyes, because I couldn't sit at all. I felt better standing up, but the pain made me very fidgety.

The doctor saw us after viewing the X-rays and said, "I don't know who told you that you had osteoarthritis, but what you have is much more serious." I'll never forget his expression; he looked so somber. "It's one of two things," he said. "It is either a tumor or a disc problem." We just looked at him. Later, Louie said that when he heard the doctor's edict, his body went cold. The doctor added, "You've got to have an MRI. Go home, and I'm going to schedule one for tomorrow morning at eleven o'clock, and then we'll see where we're going."

That night I tossed and turned and got very little sleep. I relived the same scene over and over. I kept seeing the doctor's expression when he said, "This is serious." If this is a tumor, maybe I'd had it for quite a while. Maybe I'd waited too long. I decided that if there was anything terminally wrong with me, I was going to leave the relationship. I couldn't put Louie through another experience with cancer. I simply wouldn't do that to him and Jennifer and told him so. I was determined.

That evening, Louie took Jennifer aside and said to her, "Something's wrong with Linda. I don't know what it is, but we're going to find out. She's going for an MRI tomorrow morning."

Jennifer asked, "Any idea what it might be?"

He shook his head and said, "The doctor said it was one of two things, either a tumor or a ruptured disc or some kind of disc problem."

Jennifer got upset and said, "Why is this happening to us?"

Louie tried to reassure her that we didn't know what it was yet. "But Jen," he said, "whatever it is, we're going to be there for her. Linda told me she would walk out of our lives before she'd put us through any more cancer. I told her that she isn't going anywhere, I won't let her. You know, I don't have to be married to have a commitment." Jennifer said she felt the same way. Louie was clearly worried and said, "Jen, if it's a tumor, what are we going to do?"

She said, "We're going to take care of her. There's nothing else we can do."

Throughout the night, I lay awake, curled into a fetal position. I was in excruciating pain and unable to extend my legs. As soon as I tried, the pain shot right back up again. The next morning, Louie came into my room and said, "Linda, I'm taking you to the hospital."

I said, "No, please. I'll be okay." As soon as I said that, I knew I wasn't. *I can't do this to him,* I thought. *Something's terribly wrong.*

The pain was horrible, and Louie persisted, "There's no way you're going to take the MRI this morning unless they ease your pain, and the only way they're going to do that is if you get to the hospital early and have a shot." I went along with him, because I didn't have the energy to argue. Louie tried to help me out of bed, but the pain made it impossible. He didn't waste any time calling 911, and the ambulance immediately drove me to Saint Anne's Hospital. As soon as I arrived, they gave me medication, and the pain sufficiently subsided, allowing me to be positioned in the MRI cylinder.

The technician said to me, "Okay, Linda, you have to lie real still. You can't move any part of your body. It messes up the X-ray, and we would have to take it all over again. This is going to take about forty minutes. Try to relax and don't move, okay?" I nodded, but to myself I thought, *My God, I'll never be able to do this.* For the duration of the procedure, I closed my eyes and thought, *I can do it, I can do it, oh, dear God, be with me, I can do it.* Louie was with me, standing at the end of the machine and holding my ankle. I could feel his comfort and support. What I couldn't see was that he was looking up at the ceiling thinking that if there is a God, he wouldn't be doing this to him twice. Louie knew something was clearly wrong but prayed his heart out that everything would be okay.

I came out of the MRI, and we went back to the emergency room to wait. About fifteen minutes later, the doctor came in and said, "Linda, looking at your X-ray, I see that you have a herniated disc, a ruptured disc that needs to be taken care of right away. This is bad."

I cried out in relief, "Oh, no, it's not!" I had tears in my eyes, and I was smiling. I couldn't believe it. Both Louie and I were crying for joy that it wasn't a tumor. We knew it was fixable and surgery would take care of it. The next day I had an appointment with a surgeon in Providence, Rhode Island, who, after looking at the X-rays, concurred with the diagnosis.

He explained, "What's causing you so much pain is

that the disc broke and chipped. A piece of the chip went down into your fifth vertebrae and is pushing into your sciatic nerve. You must be in severe pain!" He went on, "I don't perform surgery on anyone unless they really need it, but you need major surgery as soon as possible." It was scheduled a week later.

For a week, I lay flat in bed with my knees up into my chest. I was taking strong pain medication that caused me to be very sleepy, but as it wore off, the pain again became unbearable. The medication raised havoc with my digestive system, and when I did get up to go to the bathroom, the act of sitting caused horrible pain. The whole situation was very grim. I couldn't take any medication the day before the surgery, so by the time I reached the hospital my body was in terrible painful spasms. I was told to wait because there were no gurneys ready for me. I couldn't stand. I couldn't sit. I couldn't lie down. I was dying with pain. When Louie saw what was happening, he lost his patience and scolded the hospital staff.

"Look," he said, "you've got to do something for this woman. She's in incredible pain!" They did. Within minutes they gave me medication that barely touched the pain but helped me to carry on. I knew that more than anything else I wanted to get into that operating room.

The surgery went as planned, and when I regained consciousness, I was lying on my back in the recovery room without any pain. For the first time in years, I was comfortable. Within a few hours, I was taken back to my room. I had been through some serious surgery, but I was hungry and relieved. I had an incision in my back, and I knew I needed to be careful, but I was so happy.

The doctor came in and said, "You're incredible!" In my pain-free state, I was thrilled with the operation and his skill as a surgeon. He said, "I want you to know I did extensive surgery on your back. You really needed to have a lot of work done, which means you'll probably be in the hospital for the next three days." Later, after he had examined me further, he decided to release me the next morning.

I went home and quickly recovered. I believe that attitude had a lot to do with it. Every surgery is different, and everyone experiences pain differently. At the doctor's suggestion, the day I came home I ventured outside for some walking exercise. Walking was the best thing I could do to facilitate healing. I was outside when some neighbors walked by, and Louie told them I had just had back surgery. They looked at me in awe. They couldn't believe how well I looked and moved. At night, however, I woke up with intense cramps in my legs, which I had been told to expect. I stretched the leg muscles and walked more every day. Within two weeks, I was feeling fine. I had to be careful, I couldn't bend or lift, but I could move. As far as I was concerned, I had everything to live for. I was deeply in love with Louie, was profoundly loved by him, and we were getting married in three months, on October 28. There was a lot to do, which was added motivation to get well quickly.

Chapter 14

Wedding Day

Love is a gift.

We decided to marry in Fall River, where Louie's family and most of our mutual and personal friends lived. My family was some distance away, so we planned the wedding ourselves, but their participation in our very special day was precious and dear to us both. It was a labor of love, joy, lots of humor, and in the end, a true epiphany.

Louie and I worked beautifully as a team. I found myself in my element creating the wedding service, writing our vows, and planning every detail so the ceremony was meaningful and reverent. I also wanted Jennifer to be involved with the wedding preparations and delegated to her the bridesmaids' and maid of honor's dress selections. I chose three significant people for my bridesmaids: Jennifer; Denise, my niece and godchild; and Barbara, my very special friend from chaplaincy training. My sister Cora was my maid of honor.

Attentive to detail, taste, and style, Jennifer did a beautiful job choosing the dresses, and everyone looked lovely. Her participation was so important to me on a much deeper level. She, Louie, and I were creating a new family unit, a new life. The wedding was not only a celebration for Louie and me but a commencement for all three of us as we embarked on this uncharted journey together.

I knew what I wanted for a wedding dress and asked my dear friend Ana to help me look for it. I recall how she could not help smiling at the idea of outfitting an ex-nun for her wedding. We went to a number of stores in the area, and I fell in love with a dress in an East Providence bridal shop. Speaking from experience, Ana said, "Linda, I know you want this dress, but you need to continue until you've gone to all the bridal stores before you make your decision." I agreed, but that was tough. I went through the ordeal of going to all the shops, but I'd already made up my mind and knew the dress I wanted. As I had expected, we finally returned to East Providence and settled on the exquisite off-white, A-shaped gown. The short veil was the perfect understated accent. I felt such intense excitement that I often felt like pinching myself to make sure I was not dreaming. Ana was almost as elated as I was.

Planning the wedding set a lot of things in motion—a joyous momentum was gathering speed and I wanted everything to be perfect. I wanted the symbolism of the ceremony to be meaningful, and I wanted the important people from both of our lives involved in all parts of the ceremony. Creating a sacred environment for speaking our vows, and an atmosphere of love for those sharing the day with us was critically important. We chose my dear friend, Father George, to officiate at the Mass and the exchanging of vows. I asked another close friend, Eletha, an Episcopal priest, to read the gospel and serve as homilist. We wrote our own vows and chose the readings, the music, and the organist. The choir was made up of very supportive and loving friends who loved to sing and whose beautiful voices moved and touched everyone.

Linda's Wedding Day, October 28, 1995

On the day of the wedding it rained, but in between some hefty showers, the bridesmaids, my brother Charlie, and I got to the church on time. My younger brother shuffled his feet a little as he waited to walk me down the aisle. As it was the first time he'd ever given someone away in marriage and it was the first time I'd ever been married, we were both quite nervous. When all the bridesmaids and maid of honor had walked slowly down the aisle, Charlie turned to me and said, "Linda, are you ready for this moment?"

Brother Charlie walking Linda down the aisle on wedding day.

I looked at him and said, "I couldn't be more ready. This is the day I've been waiting for. Let's do it!" He smiled, presented his arm, and we stepped into the church. I couldn't believe how many wonderful people were there to celebrate with us. There were family members, many friends, sisters from the community, hospital staff, patients, about two hundred people in all. The church reverberated with love, and I thought the walk down the aisle would take forever, but it seemed as though, from the moment I kissed Charlie and took the arm of the man with whom I wanted to spend the rest of my life, my heart spilled over with love, excitement, and an immense readiness to accept the challenges as well as the blessings of being Louie's wife.

We also wanted Debbie's parents, Mary and Sid, to take part in the service. At the offertory they came forward with the bread and wine. Jennifer joined them and brought one yellow rose, representing Debbie, which she placed on the altar. Debbie had loved yellow roses, and whenever she was in the hospital, Louie made sure they were placed prominently in her room. The rose Jennifer brought to the altar symbolized her mother and what she had meant to her family. Following communion, a soloist sang "Ave Maria," and Louie and I took the yellow rose to the altar of the Blessed Mother. We knelt and said a brief prayer. It was an emotional time for both of us, a very symbolic moment of remembrance and thanksgiving for Debbie. At the end of the liturgy, we gave that beautiful, single, yellow rose to Debbie's parents. We knew they were happy for us, but it was also very difficult for them. Debbie had been their only child, and they missed her terribly. Our marriage made the loss more final.

Within the service, once again I lived the power of the spoken vow, but this time, I stood with my beloved, Louie. The love and support of those present was a precious blessing. I wondered, *How can we ever thank these people for joining us for such a joyous and precious moment?* Speaking our own vows and voicing our life commitment to each other only served to heighten the experience. Our rings symbolized a circle of love and the promise to protect that love, no matter what life would bring us. I'll always cherish the special memory of Louie taking my hand and together walking back up the church aisle as man and wife. I had finally come home.

Because of the rain, the receiving line formed at the end of the church. Our guests were asked to remain afterward, because we had one more surprise for them. There were so many people offering their congratulations and lots of people to kiss and hug. It was wonderful! When we'd seen everyone, we moved to the front entrance of the church. Our guests were talking, milling around, wondering what was going to happen. A woman we'd met two weeks before approached us as we'd planned. She carried a large square object that was covered with a white silk cloth. The three of us smiled at each other. She said, "Are you ready?"

We both nodded and said, "Yes!" She pulled back the cloth, revealing a beautiful white cage with large white bows on either side and inside two pure white doves.

From the time Cheryl first appeared with her precious cargo, people began to whisper. "What's this? What's going on? What's happening?" Someone held the cage as Cheryl opened the door and handed Louie and me each a dove. Over and over we heard, "Oh, my God, look at this!" "Doves, do you see that? They've got doves! I can't believe it!" Everyone was so excited. Cheryl stepped back and gave the count. On the count of three, Louie and I raised our arms over our heads and let the doves fly. It was a transcendent moment for all of us. For me, the doves in flight symbolized freedom and a new beginning. It was a sign of the release of the life I had lived and honored, and the acceptance of the blessings of our new life together; two very different yet equally precious faces of love. The doves circled the church and then headed for home. Louie and I did the same. We were now each present in the heart of the other; we were finally home.

Every minute of the reception will always remain indelibly imprinted in my memory. The festivities began with a toast from Louie's brother, Fred, who was also the best man, and Cora, my sister and maid of honor. One never knows what to expect from Fred, but it was heartwarming and funny. "Please join me," Fred said, "in toasting the four Ls—Linda, Louie, Laughter, and Love. God bless."

Cora was handed the microphone and said, "I had prepared a long speech, but after running around after Linda's train all day, I've worn myself to a frazzle, so I'll keep it short. I want to let you know we love you both very much. Louie, we welcome you to our family as our brother-in-law and, not only did we gain a brother-in-law, but also a niece, Jennifer. Jennifer, welcome to our family." Everyone applauded as Jennifer (and Louie!) beamed.

The party proceeded in a happy blur of traditional wedding activities. We danced, laughed, and celebrated with the love and camaraderie of friends and family. All too quickly, the time came to change clothes and leave the reception. We returned to the hall where they introduced us again as Mr. and Mrs. Louis Pestana. We stepped into the hall to a standing ovation, and the band played what we chose as our last song by Anne Murray, "Can I Have This Dance." As we began to dance, Jennifer ran out of the crowd, grabbed us both, and danced with us. She had tears in her eyes and was smiling as I'd never seen before. Then Jennifer and I embraced, Louie backed away, and we danced. My heart was filled with so much love and gratitude I thought it would explode with sheer joy. Louie joined us, and the three of us finished the dance together. I'll never forget those wonderful moments. Louie marveled at how spontaneous and unexpected everything had been since we first fell in love. Nothing had ever been predictable about our life together, nothing.

Big day: Lou, Jenn, Linda

We said our good-byes to everyone, thanking them for being there and sharing our day with us. There were more hugs and more tender moments. As we stepped outside, we

Lou & Linda leaving for Honeymoon

realized it had stopped raining, the sun was shining brightly and a beautiful rainbow stretched across the afternoon sky. I knew God had blessed our union.

The limousine was waiting for us, and we asked the driver to take us to the home of a very dear friend before taking us to Boston. Annelle was the last surviving member of the cancer support group, Footsteps, and she had become a very special friend to both Louie and me. Annelle and her husband, Ron, had planned to attend the wedding, but Annelle had been hospitalized a few days before and was too weak to come. Ron and their three children greeted us at the door, and Louie asked the driver to take the children on a nice long ride. We had a wonderful visit with their parents, and we later learned that Annelle had made a Herculean effort to dress and come down the stairs before we arrived. Our precious time with her was spent talking, laughing, and crying together. It was the last time we saw her. When we returned home from our honeymoon ten days later, Annelle had passed away.

After leaving our friends, we drove to Boston, where we spent the night. The following day was my forty-seventh birthday. Louie and I flew to Grand Cayman for four days and then to Aruba for another six. One day while in Aruba, Louie brought me to Costa Linda, where he said, "I'd like to show you where I stayed the last time I was here." I knew this was important to him because Aruba was one of the last places he had taken Debbie. We walked into a hotel lobby, got on the elevator, and went to the third floor. We stepped onto an open balcony and saw other hotels below separated by beautiful arrangements of flowers, shrubs, and palm trees. There were outdoor Jacuzzis shrouded by larger shrubs that made private and peaceful places. We walked along the balcony together, turned a corner, and came to a room. Louie said, "This is the room that Debbie and I stayed in." We walked to the end of the balcony to a beautiful view of the beach. We looked out over the water, and then we both saw it. With tears in our eyes, we reached for each other's hand. Neither one of us said a word. In the distance a cluster of dark clouds gathered and next to them, a beautiful rainbow.

Chapter 15

Inner Voices

Heaven knows what we need!

Family: L to R Lou, Linda, Jenn, and Jon

Time has passed, and many blessings encircle my life. Since 1995, my world has taken many memorable turns. Who I am is enough. I am here on this earth for a reason and a purpose. Life is an everyday journey, the answer to getting up each morning and facing each day. Living life is an experience that has called me to make some hard decisions and live courageously with the consequences, both good and bad, of my choices. Facing my fears head-on, unafraid of the demons I may confront, with the understanding that they are also life's gift calling me to grow and to live every moment.

The choices have been mine either to shut down or open up wide enough to experience the richness of the moment, to truly listen to my own authentic voice and to believe that all things in life shift and change and that wounds do heal and hearts do mend.

God continues to remind me of the preciousness and value of each person in our lives. On December 30, 1999, while storing Christmas decorations in the loft of the garage, my husband fell from an eight-foot ladder. Hitting his head on a wooden beam, he was unconscious when he plummeted to the concrete floor below. In that split second, as I looked down at the love of my life, unconscious, not breathing, and bleeding profusely, my life seemed to stop. If I were to help him, I had to remind myself to breathe. I called 911, all the while pleading, *Oh my God, help me!* This single moment stopped me cold and reminded me to take no one and nothing for granted, reminding me how precious each moment is and that life can change in an instant. Somehow we gather the strength to do what needs to be done. The ambulance arrived, and Lou was taken to the hospital, conscious but unaware of what was happening.

Lou survived the horrific fall protected and cushioned by a higher power.

The trauma of this moment is a constant reminder to me to stand perfectly still and reflect on the deeper question that somehow summons profound answers from within. Human relationships are sacred, a realization that has touched my soul with the strong desire to value people more and things less. I need to listen and perhaps more importantly hear the hearts and voices of those we love.

Our beautiful daughter, Jennifer, had experienced many turning points in her own journey since 1995. She has walked gingerly down her own path of loss and grief, facing the profound pain of losing her mom to breast cancer. Subsequently, she was confronted with the choice of opening her heart and allowing another woman to enter her dad's life or not. With what mixed emotions did we face this amazing challenge! I wanted to be there for Jennifer, but I also wanted to give her the time and space she needed to allow her own feelings to crystallize. The journey through her loss and grief took more than time; it took healing, understanding, and unconditional love, a love that would allow her to work through the pain emerging a capable and treasured woman in her own right. Walking with Jennifer during this fragile time was a real challenge for both Louie and me. My silent prayer for Jennifer was that she would allow herself to feel every emotion. Sadness, fear, joy, grief, loneliness and perhaps most importantly, love had allowed me to experience life at its fullest and richest. I truly believe that love blesses and heals the heart, bringing fresh blood into one's soul and melting into understanding and wisdom.

One day, Jennifer said to me, "Linda, I only hope that I

can find someone just like my dad." Shortly after that, she came to me with a big smile. "I think I have found that special person. I know I have." In December, she met Jonathan, her true soul mate. What a gift for her. In 2003, Jennifer and Jonathan were married. Watching them grow and unfold their own unique gifts and talents is a gift to her father and me.

Jennifer's Wedding Day, Linda, Jenn, Lou

On Mother's Day 2005, Jenn and Jon came for dinner. Jenn passed me a card. I had already received a card from her, so I wasn't quite sure what it was. I opened the card and noticed that it said "What is a Grandmother?" I immediately said to Jenn, "Honey I think that this is the wrong card." She told me to open it, and when I did, it said "Love, Baby Black (see you in nine months)." *Oh, my God!* I looked at Jenn and Jon, all of us weeping with joy and excitement.

This was the moment that we had been waiting for; I was thrilled beyond words. Our daughter was going to have a baby. She then asked me if I would like to be with her at the time of delivery. I cried tears of joy. I felt so honored, loved, and trusted. I truly felt like a mom. That is a blessed moment I shall never forget.

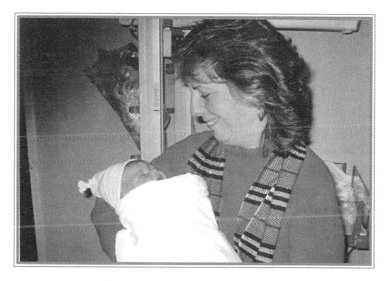

Mimi & Baby Julia Ann, January 10, 2006

Our little Julia was born on January 10, 2006, and I am now a grandmother, one of life's most precious blessings. I will always remember the first time she was placed in my arms. I looked down into Julia's little face, and I just knew I was holding an angel. She can turn inner clouds into brilliant sunshine. Lou and I could not be happier. From the very first moment I held Julia, I loved to sing to her, "You are my sunshine, my only sunshine..." Now, three years old, Julia sings along with me. I have always ended the song with "and please don't take my Julia away." Julia now adds, "And please don't take my Mimi away." At first, I cried, and now I smile with such pride!

One walks each day holding onto each experience and realizing the power of their influence. Each morning, when we wake up, we can choose to complicate or simplify our lives. The choice is up to us. The choice was up to me. Letting go of old expectations, demands, and judgments has liberated me. They no longer own my soul. I am my own person, if I so choose.

A very special friend taught me much about life, about choices, and about trusting in each moment. Collette was born with cerebral palsy. I first met her at the hospital where she volunteered her time in Pastoral Care. It is amazing how we immediately know when we have met someone who has that special charisma, someone who is authentic and loving. Collette holds and shares one of life's greatest gifts: joy. She radiates with the power of joy and love. Each day, she chooses to live life to its fullest, never complaining or feeling any self-pity, a living example of how others inspire us to live our lives with meaning and purpose.

In early 2002, I was diagnosed with fibromyalgia, a chronic condition that causes fatigue and pain in muscles and ligaments. Before being diagnosed, I felt a gripping fear for what the future might hold. After my diagnosis, I felt as though I could handle anything, because I knew that this thing called fibromyalgia would not kill me. I choose each morning to get up, to move, and to keep going. Some days are easier than others.

Chronic illness can shatter your world. It enveloped me, exhausting my energy and my thoughts. I felt exposed, vulnerable, and helpless. I do not like to depend on anyone, wanting to be capable and in control. I wanted to do things for myself. I screamed from within, "Why is this happening to me?" Then, at a calmer moment I thought, *but, then again, why not? This is an opportunity to reshape my life—to choose to move over and let God take control.* I believe that God works within and through our bodies. I paid close attention to my pain and its many causes, allowing this experience to lead me somewhere new. An awareness that has shaped my soul to realize that, through pain, we choose either to hold onto what we cannot change or to accept what is. Being vulnerable does not mean being weak, but rather inspires an inner strength resulting in the ability to remain open to new experiences and learning. How easily I forget this gift of power always attempting to shield myself from hurt, pain, questions, doubts, and risks.

In June of 2007, my oldest sister Carol was diagnosed with stage-four lymphoma and bone cancer. How would I survive another loss? I watched as Carol walked the path of acceptance and opened the door to dealing successfully with the inevitable. One afternoon, while sitting with Carol, I asked her to share with me what she would like to leave behind for her children and grandchildren. I did not want her message to go unspoken. She looked into my eyes and said, "Linda, this is what I want to leave behind for my family…" She then stated three insights very clearly, simply and lovingly:

"I want my children to always remember that I love them oh so much, that they are my lifeline and my treasures. Always remember the value of family and remain close and caring to one another. Remember that even though I am not with you, I will be with each of you in spirit. I will reach out and take care of you."

And lastly she said, "Thank you all for all that you have given to me … for the millions of memories that we have shared. They shall forever be remembered. Please never forget me." With tears in my eyes, I promised Carol that I would share this message with the family.

Six months later on December 8, 2007, with her five children around her bed, my sister Carol died in my arms. Death stings, penetrating each pore of our being. The days that followed were filled with relief that Carol was no longer suffering, but the painful reality was that Carol no longer was with us. Our hearts were deeply touched with many emotions. The love and support from family and friends was such a testimony to Carol and the love that she left behind.

Shortly after my sister's passing, a very dear friend, who was also a former sister of St. Joseph, became terminally ill with breast cancer. She was very happily married with three beautiful children. The knowledge of Marie's illness was a shock. Marie and I talked openly about where she was going and how all the people that had loved her and touched her life would be waiting for her to welcome her home. I asked her to promise me that when it was my turn to pass from this life that she would be there waiting for me. Marie assured me that she would be at the head of the line. I cried. Marie's life ended, but the legacy of her love will live on forever. Marie taught me to focus, not on yesterday, but on the "here and now." I know that my purpose here on earth is to live each and every day to its fullest.

Throughout my journey I have been so blessed to have tasted life's darkness realizing that, without the darkness, one does not appreciate the real gift of light. We do not find wholeness in life until we are willing to enter our own broken, empty places and confront them honestly. We do not find God's presence without first feeling God's absence.

From every loss emerges the lesson that now is all we have. It matters not what happened yesterday but what we carry with us into today and tomorrow. What mark do you want to leave behind? Make a choice, believe in yourself, and know that you are loved as you are, the way you are. Remember that you are enough. I once read that enough is not a condition, it is a choice. Be awake, and stand up to today, do not roll over and pretend that your life doesn't matter. Each one of us blesses others, leaving behind an indelible mark.

God is with us always. Choose to feel his presence. Choose to know how much you are loved, unconditionally. Seek to find the wisdom inside yourself. It is there, even though we are often too nearsighted to realize it. Listen to your heart and let your soul bless you in return.

Jonathan, my little sunshine Julia, Jenn

Chapter 16

To the reader, a message of love

Since telling my story, I have received one of the greatest gifts of all. The following is a letter to me from Jenn. It represents the assertiveness necessary to cross the paradox that separated us. Step by step we have both learned not only to embrace each other, but to hold, listen, and share in both the tears and the laughter, for they are moments to hold tucked in your heart forever.

Love is not a prerequisite to truth and honesty but rather a privilege accompanying its purpose. Jenn put her heart and soul into sharing with me her love and acceptance. Without giving up the legacy of her mother's love, she found that there was room in her heart to accept the role that I could play in her life, allowing the connection between us to be nurtured into the warm and comforting glow of love.

Jenn is a gift that has enriched my life, a testimony to the fact that wonderful things do happen and have happened to me! To this day, reading Jenn's letter, as I do so frequently, still brings me to tears.

With her permission, I share with you my most precious gift, the message of her love:

Linda,

I'm at a loss for words right now. My initial reaction after completing the book was: I closed it, stared at the cover, and then it happened—I cried. I don't mean my eyes filled up, I mean, I bawled my eyes out. It makes me overjoyed to know that you are happy with the most wonderful man in the world.

I cried for everyone in your story: for your mom, your dad, your memere, your sisters, your brothers, my mom, my dad, and above all for you. I cried for you, Linda—for your happiness, your sadness, your fear, everything you felt.

What an unbelievable journey you went through. Many times I placed myself in your shoes in the story. I never could have gone through what you went through. You are such a strong person. No matter what road you pursued, God was with you.

Many people feel that God lets them down. I know I did when my mother died. I immediately blamed God, asking constantly, "Why?" I didn't know what to ask, only why? I have come to realize that God is mysterious—our whole life is a mystery. Not one of us knows what is in store for us. I guess that's when the saying "Take one day at a time" really rings true.

Linda, I admire you for all your strength, love,

and the support you have given to me. I hate to think what my life would be if you had not filled the void in my family. It scares me. There are days when I have to stop my mind from thinking, *What if she never came into our lives? What if...*

You are here to stay, but sometimes it seems too good to be true—too good to be true that I have a new friend, a new mom, and a new family.

I'd like to thank you for letting me read your story. I found it very moving and powerful, and so will a lot more people. I keep my fingers crossed that it gets published, for it is such a beautiful story that will enlighten so many people's lives.

Linda, I strongly feel the presence of God and all the loved ones we have lost, and I eagerly await the answers that only He can provide.

I love you,

Jennifer

The gift of life is so precious. Every person who touches our lives blesses our hearts and touches our very soul, making a mark on our inner being.

To be called Mother, Mom, or Mommy is one of life's greatest blessings. The awe of teaching and empowering a child to grow and become his or her own person is both a true blessing and an awesome responsibility.

Jenn is now a mother and she writes this message of love to her three-year-old daughter, Julia. Because I honor

Jenn's words and am privileged to call her my daughter, I have asked her permission to share with you her words.

My love for you, Jenn and Julia, is the fuel that ignites the importance of time spent together. I want you both to know that your love wraps around me like a warm, protective blanket.

The following is Jenn's message to Julia:

My dearest Julia,

Where would we be, who would we be if life had not dealt us this amazing hand? As I look back, I know I would not be the person I am today had I not experienced all that has happened. I recall the feelings I had about life after Grandma Debbie died. I was lost, buried in a sea of grief and sorrow. I know now that what people say after such a painful loss is really quite true, "We don't get over this, we simply get through it." We survive then, slowly, and with time and love, the pain mellows and learning and maturing begin. I evolved from a scared and naïve teenage girl into a strong, confident woman, wife, and mommy for you.

Since Mimi came into our lives, we have not only gained a friend but another mother for me and a wonderful grandmother for you, not a replacement for Grandma Debbie, but a wonderful addition, someone who has opened our eyes to the warmth and joy of life after loss. Through my life experiences and her comforting ways, I have learned that we only get one chance at this thing we call Life. Because of the woman she is and the one she has helped me to become, a mutual respect and admiration has grown between us. Together, we set out on this incredible journey. Initially, it was one of pain, hurt, and anger, but, eventually as healing took hold, we have both worked tirelessly on our relationship, never giving up on each other.

I am where I am because of the choices I have made. I had to choose between being bitter about the hand I had been dealt or accepting it as a challenge and an opportunity to learn and grow. Looking back, I feel quite proud of the choices I've made, but in no way could I have done it on my own. I have a wonderful, supportive and loving family to thank. With Mimi's and Papa's help and love, I was able to choose to accept what life dealt me and live with an open heart.

In September 2003, I married your amazing daddy, becoming a devoted and supportive wife to my life's love. In January 2006, I experienced the joy of giving birth to you, my precious girl. From the moment I saw you, my heart sparkled like a twinkling star, and I cherish every day I have with you and Daddy.

Thanks to the love and patience of Papa, Mimi, and my family, I treasure this precious life with the understanding that it passes by far too quickly. It is to you, my sweet Julia, that I leave these life's lessons.

I am forever your devoted and loving

Mommy

Epilogue

Coming home

Encouragement from others clearly triggered interest in writing this memoir, but there was so much more. I hungered for awareness and understanding of all that had happened, and I wanted to share this journey of self-discovery. I knew, however, I'd need help. My thoughts and emotions carried the overwhelming fullness of my experiences of the past few years, and I was bursting but void of expression as I ached to tell my story in written words. Talking about it was one thing. Letting it flow out of a pen was quite another. With much help and reflection, the written word has become a beautiful conduit from my soul to the open hearts of all who read it.

Gently and firmly hundreds of questions came forward, the tender threads of painful details unearthed from the depths of my soul. However, there were just as many moments of encouragement, support, laughter, and unwavering confidence in my memories.

Reflecting has forced me to view myself differently and to listen to my heart more attentively. The core of understanding who I was no longer existed. As a result of translating this mélange of memories into the ordered discipline of written language, a full transformation has occurred, simultaneously making it necessary to dive slowly and deeply within myself in order to experience growth where it would truly make a difference. Ambivalence, confusion, fear, and uncertainty about the past permeated the process.

I'd often encouraged people to look at their life as a "faith journey." It was important to find and touch the power of faith, the power that carried one when one felt unable to take the next step. For me, that power of faith was a wordless state, a state beyond belief. Faith simply was. I'd experienced this power when I was in the throes of making the toughest decision of my life, the choice to leave religious life. I was alone in trying to translate the voice of my heart. Within the struggle, I became keenly aware that the image I had of myself was dying a slow death. Faith, a part of my soul beyond the image of my shattered and broken self, gave me strength when I thought I couldn't take another breath. Faith dispensed frequent reminders to just breathe, in and out, one at a time.

The experience of a greater power carried me when my world and the image of who I thought I was lay broken and dying before my eyes. Beneath the softened voice of a dying image, the voice of my heart finally emerged, and the choice of a lifetime was made.

Searching the "basement" of my heart meant that I could no longer run. While the process became intensely suffocating, it progressed into the most exhilarating and liberating experience of my life. I faced the darkness and the void of terrible emptiness built from decades of fearing what other people would think. I needed to listen, to go down those basement stairs, uncover and open the trunk, finally confronting the reality that fear had shaped my religious image.

When the discovery was made, the healing began. The lifeblood of self-awareness flowed through my heart and soul with greater ease and gentleness. I felt the true spirit of the person I was, and who I was meant to become. It gave me new energy and new life, and I breathed again in a different way.

Outwardly, however, it was utter chaos and anxiety. It was hard to make decisions for a new life when people I loved and who loved me seemed unaware of my need to move forward. "Linda, take more time. Don't go," they said. Through gritted teeth, my heart held its course. I listened to my spirit and did what I needed to do. I heard my soul whisper a call from somewhere beyond what I'd always known.

My journey might have ended there, but Louie came into my life, and the transformation of love took a giant step forward. God graced me with this gift, this mystery of falling in love at the most crucial and fragile point in my journey. It was a gift that happened and a mystery that unfolded into healing.

During the time I'd been with Louie and Debbie, I saw the emotional pain and anguish Louie endured and how very much he loved his wife. He lost a very important piece of his soul when she died. I didn't experience the loss of Debbie in the same way he did, but I felt his pain, and, when I left religious life, he felt the pain I experienced. We each allowed the other to experience our brokenness, our grief, without questions or expectations. This is how we loved each other, and this is how we healed one another.

Time has passed, and Jennifer, Louie, and I continue to learn and stretch as individuals and as a family. Louie and I have enjoyed our share of marital bliss, growing pains and all. Yet every day, we cherish the moment, the preciousness of life, and the gift of each other. Death and loss have taught us to love enduringly and well.

Having lived fervently and with loving dedication as a sister of St. Joseph for twenty-five years, I believe in turn, God allowed me to taste and touch a love that was waiting for me. Love blesses and love heals.

Much of the painful difficulty in confronting my own personal reality, I believe, has to do with shame for all the painful events my family had to live through and shame for my feelings of inadequacy and helplessness to fix it. Shame camouflaged learning and growth holding me prisoner. I became masked with an identity that wasn't real until it could no longer be disguised.

Having given birth to this book, I find myself in a very different place in my journey of self-discovery. When I first began, there were many voices, and I had to listen attentively to my authentic inner voice. It has taken time, and I've had to be very patient and gentle because the voice was very fragile. I've seen ever so clearly that no one is to blame for their "brokenness" and that with time and hard work we can "put Humpty Dumpty back together again." My story, my faith journey, has woven my brightest as well as my darkest moments with an invisible cord of faith. My birth of "self" remains an ongoing evolution and blessing. Today, I know I am good enough, kind enough, and loving enough because I've finally come home.

Family Picture: Jenn, Lou, Jon, Julia, Linda

Author Bio

Linda Lambert Pestana spent years working with individuals, helping them come to terms with their personal stories. It was this background, as well as several life-altering decisions, that led her to explore her own. Through writing her story, she reached a sense of self-fulfillment and gained peace through self-forgiveness. She hopes that her journey will help others carry out their own.

Linda received her master's degree in creation spirituality from Holy Names College in Oakland, California, and furthered her studies in clinical pastoral education at the Interfaith Healthcare Ministries in Providence, Rhode Island. She is a certified bereavement facilitator, and received certification for spiritual direction from the Mercy Center of Colorado. She is best known for designing successful retreat experiences for groups of all sizes interested in personal empowerment and healing. She lives in Swansea, Massachusetts with her husband, Louis.

Trust your heart and listen gently. I would love to hear from you.

You can reach me by writing to

Linda Pestana,
184 Kispert Court,
Swansea, MA 02777,

or by e-mail at
llpestana@aol.com

or through my Web site at
llpestana.tatepublishing.net.

listen|imagine|view|experience

AUDIO BOOK DOWNLOAD INCLUDED WITH THIS BOOK!

In your hands you hold a complete digital entertainment package. In addition to the paper version, you receive a free download of the audio version of this book. Simply use the code listed below when visiting our website. Once downloaded to your computer, you can listen to the book through your computer's speakers, burn it to an audio CD or save the file to your portable music device (such as Apple's popular iPod) and listen on the go!

How to get your free audio book digital download:

1. Visit www.tatepublishing.com and click on the e|LIVE logo on the home page.
2. Enter the following coupon code:
   a345-6764-a086-e522-e85e-ac16-271c-8042
3. Download the audio book from your e|LIVE digital locker and begin enjoying your new digital entertainment package today!